Reliance Road

(a memoir)

Kate Winn

Photos and illustrations provided by the author.

Published by
HenschelHAUS Publishing, Inc.
www.henschelHAUSbooks.com
Milwaukee, Wisconsin.

Please contact the author through the publisher.

ISBN: 9798998725258
LCCN: 20255942571

Printed in the United States of America.

Dedicated to my mother,
Margaret Ann Rasmussen Winn

TABLE OF CONTENTS

FOREWORD

In *Reliance Road—A Memoir*, Kate Winn has skillfully depicted her childhood growing up on a small Wisconsin dairy farm. Early on, she learned the attributes of being someone others could rely on and could trust to complete her chores. Life on the farm was not easy, and yet, many times, Kate was able to find enjoyment in the simple life—traipsing through the fields with her devoted dog Sissie, serenading the cows with a second-hand saxophone, or participating in local fairs with Princess, a two-ton Holstein cow.

She shares stories of attending high school in rural Whitewater, where her mother taught home economics for 23 years. She was also caught up in the student anti-war protests at the University of Wisconsin–Madison, where she studied journalism. We learn about her early days in jobs with the state government and later, in Washington D.C., where she worked in the House of Representatives and the White House on energy-related issues. Then she headed for the private sector as a lobbyist for a Fortune 500 oil and gas company. After that, she established her own government relations (GR) consulting firm. All the while, she coped long-distance with her mother's declining health in Wisconsin.

Join Kate as she journeys through her life along Reliance Road. You'll be glad you did.

—*Kira Henschel, editor and publisher*

LIVING ON RELIANCE ROAD

I grew up in the 1950s on a 125-acre dairy farm in southern Wisconsin located along a one-mile, two-lane road called Reliance. I lived there with my parents, my older sister Diane, my brother Robert, and my sweet black and brown dog, Sissie. My father was a small dairy farmer who worshiped his 25 Holstein cows and his crops. In addition to being a farmer's wife and mother, my mother taught home economics for 23 years at the Franklin Junior High School in Whitewater, three miles from our farm.

Nestled among rolling hills, Whitewater had only one stop sign along Main Street. Its population was approximately 5,000, including part-time students at the local college. Life spun no faster than a Burpee seed sign at the intersection of Highway 12 and Reliance Road.

POLITE MIDWESTERNERS

As true Midwesterners, locals minded their own business and were respectful of their and others' privacy. Everyone was polite; no one really stood out. Locals moved around in clearly marked paths. Should a neighbor stray outside the confines of the well-defined white picket fences, he would still be served at the bank counter or at the IGA store. However, in subtle ways, he might be set apart. There would be more space between him and his fellow parishioners in the pew the following Sunday. People would still say hello as he sat down, but a thin veil hung between him and the rest of the town folk.

Locals attended church regularly, cared about their children's welfare, and cheered Whitewater sports teams.

We never locked the doors to our house even when we went to town to watch a Friday night football game, attend our Methodist church, or go to a Democratic party meeting. Men wore bib overalls to funerals, and clean bowling shirts were appropriate wedding attire.

In that time, the country was catching its breath after World War II and farmers were beginning to prosper due to record agriculture production and prices.

We all have a story or two about our families, don't we? They can make us proud or they can embarrass us. They can bring happiness or surprises. They can make us angry. Most of all, they try their best.

My mother's strength, courage, and reliance taught me to speak up and make my decisions based on my own knowledge and values.

This book is a tribute to my mother. I will forever be grateful for her influence on my life.

ANCESTRY

MY MOTHER, MARGARET ANN RASMUSSEN

Margaret Ann Rasmussen was born February 13, 1918, in a small, southeastern Wisconsin town called Pleasant Prairie. Her father Robert had immigrated to Wisconsin from Denmark in 1903 at the age of 21; he joined his brother Matt, who had immigrated alone at 16.

Eventually, Matt was financially able to establish his own company and worked hard to became a successful vegetable farmer near Kenosha, Wisconsin. He started the Somers Produce Company, which shipped more than 1,500 railroad carloads of cabbage across the United States annually. The company also shipped onions and potatoes. Matt became known as the "Cabbage King." Robert managed the transportation and sale of all the produce.

My grandfather's trunk when he immigrated from Denmark
It even had wheels!

Robert married Sophia, a local girl, when he was 34. She was 30. They had two daughters—my mother and her younger sister Evalyn, "Evie." My mother was two-and-a-half years old and Evie was one when Sophia died on January 6th, 1920, while waiting for a thyroid operation.

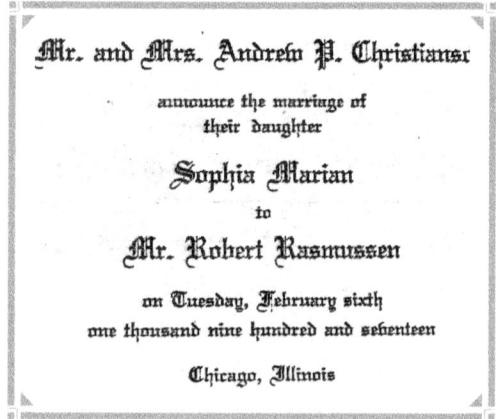

> **Mr. and Mrs. Andrew P. Christiansr**
>
> announce the marriage of
> their daughter
>
> **Sophia Marian**
>
> to
>
> **Mr. Robert Rasmussen**
>
> on Tuesday, February sixth
> one thousand nine hundred and seventeen
>
> Chicago, Illinois

In 1932, Matt committed suicide after losing all his money in the stock market crash. He had mortgaged his 650 acres of lands and farms and had invested most of his money in the stock market, which he watched closely on a ticker tape in his office.

"Daddy was never the same after his brother died," my mother told me years later. Robert, their loving and supportive father with the round face, big ears, and warm smile, took the death of his brother very badly.

He continued to farm (on a smaller scale than his brother) and remarried several years later, providing the girls with a stepmother, Lillian. Robert died in 1965.

Off to Mama Olsen's

After his wife died, Robert realized that he couldn't take care of two little ones along with his other obligations. So, he sent my mother to live with Mama Olsen, a Danish relative and immigrant who lived two hours away. My mother stayed with her for five years. The Danish community took care of each

Robert Madsen Rasmussen,
Margaret Ann (approx. age 3,
standing), Evalyn Maria (age 1, seated)

Margaret (approx. age 5)

Lillian and Robert Rasmussen
(ca 1932 marriage)

Margaret (approx. age 10)
and Evie (approx. age 8)

other when needed. Evie stayed behind with her stepmother and father.

When she was eight years old, my mother was brought back home to teach her sister English. Evie was doing poorly in school as only Danish was spoken in the household.

Mama Olsen

Boarding-School Bound

At the age of twelve, my mother was sent to boarding school—the Racine County School of Agriculture and Domestic Economy—for high school. Robert drove one hour each way to take my mother to school on Monday mornings, and bring her back home on Friday afternoons. Evie followed my mother a year later. Their father believed that school would make his daughters "marriageable."

"When I first left for boarding school," my mother told me, "I remember looking back at my little sister. She was crying as she stood up straight next to our stepmother. She waved to me as my father drove off. I saw tears on my father's face too. I was sad and frightened."

A Popular Farmer's Daughter

According to the 1933 and 1934 *Autographs* (yearbook) entries written by my mother's classmates, she was very popular. The variety of messages gave me a peek into her life during her high school years. Even with the challenges she faced until she went away to the UW in Madison, she seemed to adjust well.

> *Dear Margaret, I'll always remember you as one good baseball player and as the Prom Queen of 1934. Your friend. Ruth Nelson.*
>
> *Dear Margaret, I'll always remember you as the kid who pepped me up more than once. Please, Margaret, stop at Honey Creek sometime, won't you? You know I must repay you in some way for your kindness. Love, Marion.*
>
> *Dear Margaret: Margaret Now; Margaret forever; Rasmussen now; but not forever. Yours until the ocean wears rubber pants to keep its bottom dry. Victor*

Hot Shots

My mother and Evie came home from college for the summers and worked in the vegetable fields, produce they sold at their farm stand. When they weren't working, they both played softball in a local girls' league for the Pleasant Prairie "Hot Shots."

Their team was ahead of its time as an organized sport. From 1935 to 1939, the team was state champion four years in a row. Most of the players lived in the Pleasant Prairie area.

My mother told me on one of our car trips, "we were just girls who enjoyed playing softball. Surprisingly, we had good crowds at our games, especially given we weren't professionals."

The Hot Shots. Evie is seated on the left.
My mother is in the middle in the back row.

"I loved being catcher and was pretty good at it, I must say. It was certainly a lot more fun than selling vegetables!" she chuckled.

Their softball days ended when Evie and my mother headed back to college. They heard later that girls who made the cut after tryouts were required by male coaches to attend charm school. They were shown how to apply makeup and get out of a car gracefully. That would not have appealed to my mother or Aunt Evie.

My Mother, Motherless

In later days, during one of my visits home, Mother and I were reminiscing about our respective lives. Somehow, the experience of being motherless arose.

I must admit that I didn't grasp the significance of her early experiences until our conversation. At a very young age, she was made aware of the fragility of human happiness. She was a half-orphan, robbed of her mother's love and of her childhood.

"You never had a mother. I couldn't imagine not having you to protect me. You've always encouraged me and told me that I could do anything that I set my mind to. I could dream big. No one taught you to dream."

Her response: "Oh, I dreamed when I read books that I kept under my bed when I lived with Mama Olsen. Books were my escape. I felt her love. Protected. That's what I remember anyway."

She sounded wistful and sat up straighter. I looked at her and instead of her usually sparkling deep-brown eyes, I saw pools of hurt and grief.

MY FATHER, JAY WINN

My father was born in 1914 and grew up in rural Iowa in a house with dirt floors. His father, Jesse, subsisted as a small farmer with one cornfield. As the story goes, Jesse and Huldah, Jay's mother, met "over the fence" when they both were working in the field.

Jesse and Huldah had five children: my father Jay; LaVern (a NASA scientist); Leonard (a veterinarian); Norris (a decorated Navy pilot), and Wilma, who became a homemaker and married a farmer.

As part of the New Deal program to help lift the country out of the Great Depression, President Franklin D. Roosevelt established the Civilian Conservation Corps (CCC), which allowed single men between the ages of 18 and 25 to enlist in work programs that aimed to improve public lands and parks.

Huldah and Jesse Winn, Jay's parents.

(L to R) LaVern, Wilma, Norris, Leonard, and Jay.

For many, just the prospect of three meals a day and a bed were enough to get young men, like my father, to enroll. As jobs were scarce, the CCC allowed them to get their first jobs. Those who enlisted earned $30 a month, $25 of which were

Jay Winn and his mother.

sent directly to their families. The other $5 were for the enrollees.

Early Days

My father was a winter-term student taking what was known as the "Short Course," a 12-week agricultural program taught over a three-year period. It was designed to assist those who didn't have the financial resources for a full four-year program, but wanted to learn how to become successful farmers.

While my father was taking classes in Madison, he was introduced to my mother by his brother Leonard. She was in her final year as a chemistry major at the University of Wisconsin.

Several months after my mother graduated, they eloped. My father was able to get a job managing a large dairy farm shortly after that. According to a letter written by my Aunt Evie to my sister Diane, my parents eloped without telling anyone but her father, who gave his blessing. My mother had fallen instantly in love with my father, who was the love of her life. He was 25; she was 21.

From letters I found while I was doing family research, my father managed several farms successfully and built a very good reputation among the larger farmers. One of his employers was Marek Weber, a renowned Austrian violinist, conductor, and bandleader, who gave up his musical career to begin farming.

Written March 9, 1948 by an acquaintance of Merek Weber's:

"... we consider you the greatest farmer we have ever met up with in these United States."

Excerpt of a letter of a previous client asking Jay for recommendations for an experienced farmer to work the land and work with the cattle.

---

* * *

One morning, when my mother was driving me to high school, she mentioned something about eloping. I don't recall why the subject came up—perhaps something on the radio. When I asked why they had eloped, my mother explained that she didn't want her father to spend money on a wedding. Years later, Aunt Evie told me that their father said that "they were going away as man and wife."

It was hard for me to think of my mother not having a proper wedding. I wondered if she was okay with that. I also wondered why she hadn't told her sister about her plans to elope. Evie shared with me that "we were never close after she married Jay. I really didn't like him...your mother and I did stay in contact. I loved her all my life, but it was different."

Had my mother felt guilty for eloping and therefore worked so hard as a farm wife and teacher? Was my mother atoning all her life? The thoughts crossed my mind.

Evie said dismissively, "Oh, he had the most beautiful blue eyes. Margaret always had that dreamy look on her face. She thought he was the handsomest man who ever walked the face of the earth."

Evie married Lester, an accomplished chemist who later held numerous patents. Like Margaret and Jay, Evie and Lester met in Madison and were married soon thereafter.

In a recent conversation with my sister while writing this memoir, I asked her if our mother had ever talked about eloping. Diane's response was terse and swift: "Never!"

Graduation day (June 1940)
Standing in front of Bascom Hall.

Margaret and Jay Winn, the happy couple.

LIFE ON THE FARM

The Winn family (L to R): Jay, Robert, my mother holding me, and Diane.
Below, our farmhouse.

OUR FARM

By 1949, my parents had saved up enough money to buy the 125-acre dairy farm on Reliance Road in Whitewater, Wisconsin for $350. My father had been managing two large dairy farms for well-to-do businessmen. Diane was nine and Robert was seven. I was on the way and was born six months after the move.

My mother was 31 years old when I was born. She called on a local midwife to help with my birth. Much later, when I was going through her papers, I found this letter that she had written to wish me a happy birthday. It was dated March 7, 1972.

> *"As I sit here, I thought of the day you arrived. There was still snow on the ground, maybe not quite as much as today. About four in the morning, you alerted me. Your father drove me to the midwife in town. If memory serves me right, you arrived about 9:20 that evening. Happy birthday. You will be in my thoughts and prayers, as you always are. You were surely special to Daddy. He had you with him most of the time. You know you are special to me too."*

Our modest white house had three small bedrooms, one bathroom and one bathtub. When the temperatures dropped below freezing on those frigid January and February nights, our thin, drafty windows offered little protection from the cold. Diane and I shivered and piled on an assortment of old wool blankets to keep warm.

Our farm on Reliance Road.

JUST MOMMY AND ME

I loved to climb into the front seat of our big white Oldsmobile with my mother, who drove us to Main Street in town, especially because she always made our times together fun.

I held her hand as I skipped beside her before we went into the IGA or A&P grocery store. She filled our basket with the things she needed to feed us every day, like sugar, flour, cooking oil, maple syrup, cans of tuna, onions, and bread and butter.

My daddy didn't go to the store very often; when he did, he would always buy candy. Of course, I liked that. My favorites were Heath bars, and I also liked Baby Ruth and MARS. The only other things he purchased were Limburger cheese and pickled pigs feet. I hated the strong, awful smell of the cheese and the gross look of the pig's feet in the glass jar. I also felt sick when I watched him eating those.

The stores weren't very big, so my mother let me go to the candy counter by myself. I would ask the man working there if I could buy a Heath bar; my mother usually gave me a nickel to pay for it. The owner knew what I liked and I always smiled back at him. "Thank you, Mr. Lewis."

Searching for "My Baby"

When the mailman delivered the big, floppy Sears-Roebuck catalogue to our house twice a year, I got excited. I asked my mother to help me find the section selling baby-girl clothes for four-year-olds like me. She let me take my time turning the pages with the toddlers and their pretty dresses. After looking through the catalogue, I eventually pointed to the baby I wanted to bring home.

One time, I told her I wanted the one with the pink bow.

"Sweetie, are you sure you like the pink dress? You already have one like that."

"No, Mommy. I want the baby!"

Of course, no baby ever came to our house.

Mommy's Hands

When I was very small, I really enjoyed sitting at our round oak kitchen table watching my mommy's hands as she mixed flour, butter, and milk together to make yummy Danish orange rolls. She tugged pieces of dough from a glass bowl and rolled them around until they were perfect spheres. Then she would place them on a greased cookie sheet. The balls of dough reminded me of little balloons. Sometimes, she would

```
OUT-OF-THIS-WORLD Orange Rolls  (Margaret Winn)

Scald - 1 cup milk

Soften - 1 pkg. yeast in
         1/4 cup warm water (110° to 115°)
         Let stand 5 to 10 minutes

Combine - 1/4 cup sugar
          3 TB. shortening
          1 tsp. salt
Immediately pour scalded milk over ingredients in bowl, and stir
          until shortening is melted. When lukewarm, blend in,
          beating until smooth
                     1/2 cup flour
          Stir softened yeast & add, mixing well.

Measure 2 1/2 to 3 cups four - add about half the flour to
          the yeast mixture & beat very smooth.  Beat in
                     1 egg, well beaten
          Then beat in enough of remaining flour to make a
          soft dough.  Turn dough onto a lightly floured surface
          and let stand for 5 to 10 minutes.  Knead - form into ball
          and place in a greased bowl - turn to bring greased surface to top.
          Cover and let rise in warm place until doubled.  Punch down &
          turn over in bowl - cover and let rise again until nearly
          doubled.  Punch down and turn out onto floured surface.

Roll out to a rectangle about 1/4 inch thick.

Combine - 3/4 cup sugar and grated rind of 2 oranges.

Spread dough with melted butter; sprinkle sugar mixture evenly over
          surface; roll up as for jelly roll.  Cut one inch slices.
          Place cut-side down in greased muffin tins or flat baking
          pan.  Cover & let rise until doubled (30 to 45 minutes).

Bake at 350° for 20 to 25 minutes.

Drizzle hot rolls with glaze mixture of 1 cup powdered sugar and 4 TB orange juice

                        ######
```

swiftly flick an ant or two out the screen door. I don't think she knew I saw her do that and I didn't say anything.

"Can I lick the bowl?"

I knew the answer, but I still asked. She always left some dough clinging to the sides of the big mixing bowl.

"Of course, you can!" she smiled, dusting flour off her apron.

One morning, when I was watching my mother and chattering away, the story of *Peter and the Wolf* was playing on our pink, plastic, second-hand record player. Right in the middle of my sentence, I blurted out, "Poor duck!" Then I went right back chatting about what I must have thought was important. Mommy loved telling that story. I was five years old.

I liked it too when she put on a big kitchen mitt and pulled steaming hot rolls from the oven. I loved the orangey smell. After the golden-brown rolls were cool enough to eat, she would spread one with butter. One of my favorite things was licking the warm, dripping, delicious butter off my hands.

In those moments, all was right in my world.

Fun at the Shoe Store

Each year, when I was ages five to eleven, before school started in the fall, my mother took me to Don's Shoe Store on Main Street to buy a new pair of saddle shoes. I loved having nice new shoes. I also liked watching my feet being measured by an x-ray machine—I could see the bones inside them when the machine lit up. The machines were popular in the 1950s. When I was much older, I learned that they emitted dangerous levels of radiation and eventually were banned.

Sometimes, when my mother went up to the counter to pay for my shoes, I scurried to a machine in the back corner and stuck in my fingers and feet and watched them glow, hoping my mother wouldn't catch me.

My Dog Sissie

I loved my dog. She was my scruffy best friend with pretty brown eyes. She was older than I was, but not by much. From the time I was old enough to be outside and around the barn, Sissie was with me.

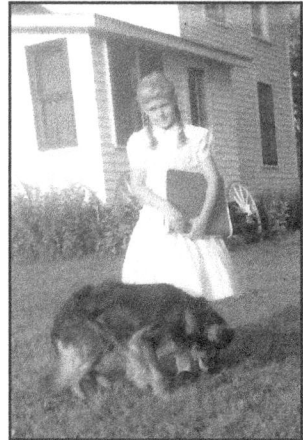

Sissie and me waiting for the school bus.

I liked the way she wagged her tail when she was happy. I called it her "happy tail." She belonged to me in my world. She walked by my side as we explored hills behind our barn, often trying to catch bunnies. We wouldn't hurt them; I just wanted to pet their soft fur. They were very cute, but they ran away from us most of the time.

Our farm was also the place where city folks and friends from church brought their pets for us to keep. I remember a horse named Vicki; a sweet black-and-white mutt called Peppy; and two small cats, Dolly and Buddy. My Aunt Evie called them "curbside cuties."

"Oh, I Wish I Were an Oscar Mayer Wiener!"

One day, I was hungry and I could tell that Sissie wanted something to eat too because of the way she looked at me. Those eyes. So we walked to our house. No one was there; everyone was in the barn doing chores.

What could we have to eat? I wondered as I looked in the refrigerator. There wasn't much to see, only carrots, beans, and potatoes from the night before.

Of course, there was fresh milk from the milkhouse. I hated it because it was thick; I refused to drink it. My fussiness made my father very angry, especially when I broke my leg slipping on some ice when I was 12 years old. I would only drink store-bought milk, which he felt was a waste of money since we had it in abundance.

The only thing I saw that Sissie would like were some Oscar Mayer hot dogs. I don't remember exactly how I did it, but I opened the package and pulled out a sausage. Sissie had a bite; I had a bite. She had a bite; I had a bite. Soon, she had eaten four; I had eaten one, and we shared the last one. Anyway, we were both full. Sissie put on her happy tail.

I heard the screen door slam as Daddy, Diane, and Robert came into the kitchen. They were all sweaty, tired, and hungry after working all day long. I was scared. Trouble was coming. I told my mother I didn't know what happened to the hot dogs, even though she hardly needed any proof that Sissie

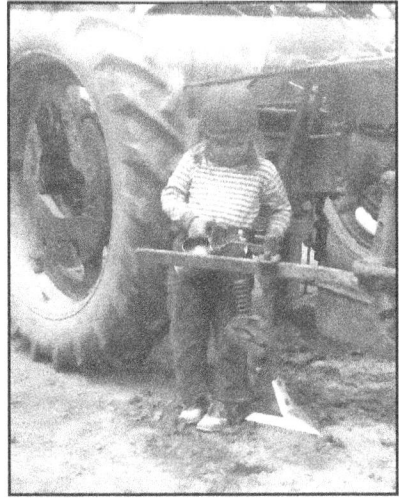

Helping Daddy fix the tractor
(approx. 4 years old).

and I had opened the package and eaten the hot dogs. Sissie's tail was wagging, the plastic wrapping was on top of the garbage container, and I was trying hard not to cry.

My parents didn't yell at me. Everyone sat quietly at the kitchen table, except my poor mother. She put on her apron and began peeling and cutting up more vegetables for supper. My sister was told to go to the garden and pick some green beans. Robert played with a spoon, looking mad. He was sitting on one foot on his chair, Daddy told him to sit up straight and told me to quit crying.

Sissie stretched out in her usual corner for a nap.

Butterflies in My Tummy—Terrified of the Piano Recital

My mother felt strongly that we three children should learn to play the piano. She had saved enough money from various jobs to buy a Chickering quarter-grand piano. She gave us all weekly piano lessons at home at first, and later drove me into

Playing the piano.

town for my weekly lessons. Most of the time, I hadn't practiced. I never improved despite Mrs. Schaefer's best efforts. She put on an annual piano recital at her home. My parents, along with others, were crowded into the living room of the high-ceilinged old Victorian that stood on a hill near the center of town. This was a chance for them to listen to their children play a favorite piece and to be proud.

When my name was called, I walked the few steps to the bench and started playing. Even though I was six years old, I was very scared and just wanted to go hide somewhere. My tummy hurt. I hated knowing that all those eyes were staring at me. It wasn't long before I stumbled and played the wrong keys. I stopped and then went back and started again at the place where I played the wrong keys. On my third try, I played the piece correctly. Everyone clapped.

Then I returned to my parents' seats and snuggled next to my mother. The piano teacher smiled and then announced that my brother was playing next. Before long, he moved his fingers around the keyboard quickly and looked like he was having fun. I knew the piece that he was playing from hearing him practice. He paused briefly and then carried on playing. Probably no one but me realized that he had missed some keys, but he just played on, improvising. A few months later, he won a state piano competition; he was a natural talent.

Eventually, my mother quietly declared defeat trying to interest me to learn the piano. My heart wasn't in it.

MY ONE-ROOM SCHOOLHOUSE

I attended first grade in a one-room schoolhouse that was a ten-minute walk from our farm along Reliance Road. I was five years old. Children from grades one to eight were packed into the dusty, dark room. We all had the same teacher, Mrs. Erdman. Her long brown hair was piled high on her head and secured with bobby pins. Some days, she had a pretty red or yellow flower in her hair. The color was nice because it stood out from the black clothes she often wore.

The youngest children—five of us—sat in the front row closest to the chalk board. Mrs. Erdman taught us grammar and how to read and write. *Fun with Dick and Jane* was my favorite reader. Our desks were made of polished wood and wrought iron. The tops lifted up so she could check to see if our desks were clean and tidy. The floor was hardwood; we all knew where she was as she limped between the rows. Her

The one-room schoolhouse.

27

black, lace-up shoes scraped along the floor as she observed her flock.

If we had to visit the outhouse, I always tried to hold it because I didn't like sitting on the wooden hole; I worried that something would bite me, so I always hurried to do what I had to do.

Best to Behave

Mrs. Erdman didn't smile much, but she did have her hands full teaching thirty-plus children. Every now and then some-one—usually one of the older boys—would break a rule. It wouldn't be long before he was told to go to the front of the room to await his punishment. Most often, recess was cancelled for the culprit, but sweeping the floor and cleaning erasers were also punishments, depending on how severely the child had disobeyed.

One day, one of the older boys got caught swearing. We all waited in silence to see what would happen. Of course, there was no place for the bad boy to hide once a rule had been broken. Mrs. Erdman pulled out a pink bonnet from her desk and told him to put it on. Then she marched him to the front of the room and made him sit between two girls. It was funny to see him; his face was very red and he looked like he was about to cry. I heard some giggling, but I sat very quietly. Mrs. Erdman was scary when she was mad.

Little Brown Pills

Mrs. Erdman gave each of us a weekly iodine tablet. I didn't like the taste, but my mother told me I had to take them so I wouldn't get a goiter. I later learned that the Upper Midwest

My class in the one-room schoolhouse.
I'm in the front row, 2nd from left in the white dress and pants.

and Great Lakes region were called the "Goiter Belt" because many people suffered from an iodine deficiency.

The Scary Vaccinations

I didn't like the taste of the pills, but I really hated getting shots, such as ones for smallpox, polio, measles, or mumps. My mother explained that the shots would keep me from getting sick, and also prevent illnesses that stalked the whole community.

I remember one time that my daddy drove me to school to get a shot. Before we left the house, I found a pen and put a tiny black spot on my upper arm. As I waited in line, I got more and more scared. I pulled off my sweater and showed the nurse that I had already had my shot. Needless to say, my ploy was unsuccessful.

My memory of this situation was that the needle broke in my arm. I do not know whether it actually did or not, but I have had a phobia of needles all my life.

Mother Sticking to Her Guns

In the early 1950s, teachers forced most children to learn to write with their right hand. Superstition surrounded left-handed people; many believed that being left-handed would bring bad luck. Teachers also thought that left-handed children would have a more difficult time in school and in life if they were different from right-handed kids.

My mother, always a progressive, didn't believe this. She didn't care what teachers or others thought. Instead, she let me be left-handed. She always told me, "You be you." And I've been left-handed all my life.

After I finished the first grade, I rode a school bus to Lakeview School, twenty minutes away, to attend second through seventh grades. I waited at the end of our driveway for the school bus driver to let me get onto the big yellow school bus. Most days, twelve other kids were picked up along the route. Sometimes the driver, an older man, didn't have his teeth in; it was hard for me not to giggle looking at his sunken mouth.

Starting in eighth grade, I rode with my mother in our white Oldsmobile to attend Franklin Junior High School, where she taught home economics. I was nervous having her as a teacher and I worried that my friends wouldn't like her. I also felt that I had to get perfect scores or risk letting her down.

LIFE WASN'T EASY

Creative in the Kitchen

I remember times when money was short and my mother and father had to "be careful." My mother told me that my father wouldn't ever admit it, but we had to watch our pennies. Just selling milk wouldn't keep food on the table.

Back then, we didn't have a microwave or packaged meals, so it took my mother time, energy, and creativity to provide two or three meals a day for three hungry kids, a husband, and herself. Most years, my father bought a side of beef that lasted throughout the winter months. Mother regularly baked dinner rolls, sauteed vegetables, and roasted beef, which was served smothered in thick gravy made with bits of the beef, milk, and flour. Mashed potatoes with pools of butter were the usual side dish. Apple and rhubarb pies just out of the oven were devoured quickly, particularly with a special treat of vanilla ice cream that melted into a gooey, delicious mess.

Mother also often mixed up a concoction of tuna, noodles, and canned soup—all stirred together to create the infamous tuna noodle casserole. As I remember, she said it was the original Betty Crocker recipe that specifically called for Campbell's Cream of Mushroom soup.

When we didn't have the ingredients for casseroles, there was always yucky liver, one of our mother's go-to entrées. She often served it because it was cheap. She was an accomplished cook and ace baker, but for some reason, sautéing liver wasn't her strong suit. It was always overcooked and looked like a worn piece of car tire. It didn't taste much better either.

The dinner table was quiet when the five of us focused on cutting our tough servings of liver into bite-sized pieces that would be easier to swallow. Pouring on ketchup helped too. Lots of it. Some nights, Mother would bring in onions from our garden and sauté them with the liver. Those dishes were called "Friday night specials."

For dessert, we could choose from a variety of Jell-O flavors. Hardly gourmet, but certainly filling.

Breakfast Rebellion

Many mornings, my mother would briskly stir a mixture of oil, flour, milk, and butter that crackled as she poured it into a hot, oiled skillet. Very quickly, the mounds of perfectly rounded batter began to bubble.

There were no breakfast surprises. Almost every morning, I quietly hoped that she might surprise us and feed us something other than pancakes. By breakfast time, we had already been up for two hours shoveling manure, tossing silage, feeding cows, and carrying pails of milk. We were tired and hungry.

One spring morning, I looked across the kitchen table and proclaimed, "I'm done. Done eating pancakes. Mother, you know I have never liked them. They're all we ever eat."

"Try putting on more syrup or butter," she said in her chipper voice.

"No, Mother. They are what they are. I said, I'm done. I don't even like the smell." At 15, this was my first conscious act of rebellion. It felt good.

The rare breakfast back-up wasn't very appealing either. Oatmeal, the clumpy stuff, was just as unappetizing as pancakes. Adding milk and sugar didn't help the oatmeal either. The lumps and glue-like consistency remained.

Radium Hazards

In addition to her duties in our kitchen, my mother began working at an electronics plant in town to earn some extra money, Factory workers applied radium paint to the tiny dials that made the watches glow in the dark. The paint was called "liquid sunshine." Radium promised to tackle various ailments, including cancer. The women were breathing it in with nearly every brushstroke. The water and radioactive radium mixture glowed. Then it started killing the workers and brought radium poisoning to national attention. In 1968, the use of radium in wristwatches was banned.

I don't know how long my mother worked at the plant before my Aunt Evie warned her of the hazards of being in an environment with radiation and urged her to quit. She did. My guess is that Evie's husband, a well-regarded chemist, was aware of the dangers of radium and shared them.

A New Dawn

Still needing to be "careful" and working outside the house to earn additional funds, my mother joined a network of home economists and teachers called "Home Electrification Specialists." They traveled to rural areas throughout the 1950s, demonstrating to housewives how to get the most out of their new electric appliances—especially ovens and refrigerators.

The program was part of a New Deal plan championed by President Roosevelt to help rural areas and farming communities modernize. Electricity and electrical appliances were commonplace in cities, but not in rural places like Whitewater and surrounding areas. As a result, many rural farm families often didn't know how to use those modern appliances and didn't appreciate their potential for making farm life easier.

My mother told me that it wasn't easy explaining the benefits of the new electric appliances to local housewives. Her teaching credentials as a home economics instructor did not open doors, as many viewed learning home economics only as training for their expected futures as wives and mothers.

No Luxuries, Home Remedies

Growing up on the farm meant saving as much money as possible. Instead of toothpaste, for example, we used a mixture of salt and baking soda.

If one of us had a "bad tummy," which I often did, a soap and warm water enema did the trick. When any of us came down with the sniffles, we heard, "Come here, Sweetie." Mother cut up onions and stuffed them into scratchy woolen socks or dish towels and draped the poultice around our necks. Mother told us that the Russians had been researching the benefits of onions for years and discovered that they help cure colds and other ailments. I didn't care what the Russians were doing.

She also had another trick up her sleeve to get rid of the common cold. She cut up onions and placed them on a plate next to our beds. As much as I hated it, to my mother's credit, her remedies usually worked. However, trying to get the smell of onions off my neck wasn't easy and was not always success-ful. More than once, classmates would walk by me at school and giggle, "Onions again?"

That stung too.

The one luxury my mother allowed herself was using Pond's Cold Cream. In the 1950s, it was considered a revolu-tionary product and one of the first cold-cream lotions on the market. It became popular because women, including my mother, loved the way it moisturized their skin. I remember her friends often complimenting her on her soft, smooth skin.

Unlike the monotonous pancakes, I grew to love onions—just not around my neck or near my bed.

The Party Line

"Party line" was an appropriate name for our telephone service. We shared our line with five other households and were all connected to the same physical phone lines. Each household had its own unique ring pattern, allowing the residents to know when an incoming call was for them.

Our neighbor, Mrs. Harrison, spent most of her days sitting on a worn-out cushion on her rocking chair listening to—and interrupting—conversations. The neighbors all knew about her curiosity and persistence so there were no secrets or privacy. When the phone rang, Mrs. Harrison already knew by the ring pattern who was calling. Often she couldn't help herself and would chime in to correct someone's version of events or to add some gossip. She was completely at ease jumping into the phone calls of others, and for instance, would correct the name of the boy who got a high school girl pregnant. "No, it wasn't the Miller boy. Some boy from out of town." She spoke with authority and always waited for the next call.

THINK IT OVER

My mother sat at our kitchen table, staring at the letter from her stepmother, Lillian. "I think your family should let you go. You have been a good wife and mother, and have earned a well-deserved vacation. Think it over and decide favorably. Lynn very much would like you to see her graduate."

Lynn was my mother's half-sister and was fifteen years younger.

Not many letters came to our farm. When they did, they often contained news about someone who was sick or who had died or about crops that had suffered from a dry spell. Sometimes a letter arrived relaying news from our Danish relatives.

"What does it say, Mommy?" I asked. (At the time, I was six years old; I called my mother "Mommy" until I was ten.)

Diane and I stared at her across our kitchen table.

"My stepmother wants me to attend my sister's graduation. Lynn is graduating with honors, studying opera at the Julliard School of Music in New York City. It's a very good school."

* * *

My Aunt Lynn had grown up working on a vegetable farm in Wisconsin. No rich person had pulled strings for her. It was her talent that had opened Julliard's doors. Her coaches praised her mezzo-soprano voice and predicted that she was destined to become a famous opera singer. She proved them correct. Later, she did become a star, singing at renowned opera houses around the world.

* * *

"Are you going?" Diane asked.

"I have to check with Daddy first. If I go, I'll fly there. She lives far away in a big place called New York City."

"Are you going to fly on an airplane?" my brother asked. "Maybe I'll see you up there flying by. I'll wave." He spread his arms as far as he could stretch and moved them up and down like a bird.

My sister gave him a "you're silly" look.

We didn't hear anything more about Mommy going away until one afternoon when she arrived home from teaching carrying a brown box with "Miller's Clothing" written on its side. Miller's was the only women's clothing store in White-water. Mother usually carried things from the grocery store in brown paper bags, but this one was different.

"Daddy said I could go, and I will be away only one night."

She smiled as she pulled out a baby-blue and tan cotton dress. "What do you think?"

"Pretty. Try it on," my sister begged, feeling the softness of the cotton.

"I'll try it on for you later. We have to get supper ready for Daddy and Robert. They'll be finished with the chores soon."

It was a hot day. My mother wiped sweat off her face with a dish cloth and quickly slipped into her comfortable shoes. Her feet often hurt from standing on the hardwood floor in her classroom all day.

When she was upset, her temples would pulse. They were doing that now. My sister looked directly at her.

"You just got a new dress. You look so sad. What's wrong?" Diane asked.

* * *

Daddy and Robert came in from doing chores. My sister and I set the table, and our mother got dinner ready. Right after she finished saying the blessing, Daddy blew his nose and asked her what time they had to leave for the Milwaukee airport the next morning. He didn't clear his plate nor have his usual seconds. He didn't even turn on the radio to listen to the *Wisconsin Farm Report* before heading outside.

Our mother ate quietly. "Anyone want seconds?" she asked. The three of us shook our heads no and continued slowly chewing our food. The only sound was the scraping of forks on plates. Robert looked across the table.

"So, you go tomorrow? When do you come back?" he asked.

"Daddy wants me to stay only one night," she said in a quiet voice.

* * *

The next morning, Daddy was already sitting in the car and honking the Oldsmobile's horn. We kids squished together at the screen door. Mommy gave us each a kiss and then put her small, brown Samsonite suitcase in the backseat.

"I love you!" She waved, her hand going back and forth until we couldn't see the car anymore. She looked so pretty with her long brown hair in a bun.

It had begun to rain so I called Sissie to sit by me as I played one of my favorite games—trying to guess which raindrops would get to the bottom of the screen the fastest. I didn't want to think about Mommy leaving us, even for a day.

* * *

I heard about this occasion much later in life.

Aunt Lynn lived on the fourth floor of a classic brownstone house without an elevator on Riverside Drive in New York City. Mommy caught her breath before she rang the doorbell.

"I'm thrilled you're here to share in my excitement! It means so much to me! Oh, I'm going to have a little weep."

They hugged each other. "I wouldn't miss this for anything, Lynn! I am so proud of you! Your singing at the Metropolitan Opera is cause for a big celebration!"

They sat next to each other on a cozy red sofa. Lynn said, "You'll be in the front row. The ceremony shouldn't be too long. After it's over, we'll go to a small club to hear an amazing singer, Etta James. We'll make it an early night; you've had a long day. We'll catch up more tomorrow when things are less hectic. Before we get ready to go, tell me, how are the children?" Lynn asked.

"Growing up too fast! Diane is about to turn thirteen. Robert is eleven, and Kay is five. The doctors finally figured out that Robert is lactose intolerant. He's eating much better now and putting on weight. Jay is good. You know he loves his cows. Always work to do on the farm. Teaching is challenging. Right now, I have eighth-grade boys. Trying to teach them how to sew on a button, boil an egg, or use the sewing machine isn't easy.

"You never complain, do you, Sis? You keep your grief inside. You're always the one who helps others and gives everyone warmth and light," Lynn said, reaching out to hold her sister's hand.

"I feel blessed. The main thing is, I have three healthy children and a healthy husband," Mommy said.

The next morning, Lynn was shocked to find out that my mother was booked on an evening flight back home that night. After her initial hesitation, Lynn convinced my mother to call home and say that she was staying one more night.

"I never thought to ask how long you're staying, but just one night is crazy! Please think it over and stay at least another one," Lynn pleaded. She didn't say it out loud, but she often felt that my father made himself feel better by not allowing my mother to feel good.

* * *

Diane was the only one at home when our mother called.

"Hello, Sweetie," Mother said in a low voice. "How's everyone? Is Daddy there? Aunt Lynn wants me to stay an extra night. With her performance, we haven't had much time to catch up."

Diane said, "No, he's not here. He's gone to the co-op. Want me to tell him you called and that you're not coming back tonight?"

"Yes. Please tell him that I'll be on the same United flight, just tomorrow night, not tonight. He can reach me at Lynn's if he needs to confirm. Love you, Sweetie."

* * *

Daddy slammed the car door and rushed past us, heading out to the barn without saying a word. The three of us ran to the back door. Mother leaned over and gave us all hugs.

"I'm so happy to be home."

We all headed inside. Mother had brought key rings with pictures of big red apples on them for my brother and sister and a small stuffed doggy with the same red apple on its collar for me. Mother explained that New York was known as "The Big Apple."

"I'll tell you all about my visit in the morning. It's late and you've already eaten your dinner. I'm tired."

"Get into bed right now," my sister hissed at me as she pushed me in the direction of the bedroom. Then she tiptoed to the bathroom. Our mother was gently rubbing Pond's on her face.

Diane whispered, "Mother, your face! It's black and blue. What happened? I just saw it from the light in the hallway. And look, your glasses are broken!"

"I was rushing to meet your father at the arrival gate. I lost my balance and fell. You know your mother can be clumsy at times. I was walking too fast when I slipped. It will be better in the morning."

The Confession

Then my mother shook her head and took a deep breath, deciding to tell Diane the truth about what had happened. "I know that Daddy was very angry because I stayed an extra night. I saw the look on his face when he met me at the airport, but to be honest, I didn't expect his burst of anger in the airport parking lot. He slapped me across my face twice; that's when my glasses fell. I tried to cover my face, but I wasn't fast enough. He will calm down, but it will take a while."

Sister Diane, me, and brother Robert.

"That's awful!" my sister shouted, then quieted down so she wouldn't wake me. "What's wrong with him? When he's mad, he even kicks his cows—and he loves them so much."

"I don't know what possesses him, but we'll get through this. I'm sorry that you had to see this, Sweetie. You three children mean the world to me. Your father raises money for our Methodist church. He works hard. He checks in with his parents when we go on Sunday afternoon car rides. He can be a good man. Let's stop now and go to bed."

FARM CHORES AND CHALLENGES

There was no time to rest on the farm; our cows had to be milked and fed twice a day and manure needed to be scooped from gutters. My sister, brother, and later I spent hours driving our old Case tractor cutting and crimping alfalfa. When those chores were done, there were always weeds to be pulled in our huge vegetable garden.

* * *

We hated the knock on the downstairs door before dawn, especially on those frigid Wisconsin winter mornings. It was time to heed our father's daily call to action and hurry along the frozen driveway to the barn.

My tattered wool mittens didn't keep my hands warm, so my fingers hurt when I tried to bend them. I would find my old, gentle cow eating her morning breakfast in her stanchion and slide my left hand between her low-hanging udder and the inside of her back leg. She was so old she never raised a leg or tried to kick. I could always count on her to warm my hands.

Daddy had already begun milking the cows. The dirty plastic radio was crackling. It was on the same farm station as usual with updates about the price of milk or pigs or something equally boring. When I was six, the *Farm Report* didn't mean anything to me.

I used a small pitchfork to carry silage from the silo to the cows lined up in their stanchions. They were always ready to eat; I liked seeing them chomp away at their morning meals. Sometimes, I had to push one's head away from her neighbor's as she tried to snatch some of the other cow's food.

The Baby Calf is on Her Way

"Did you look in the pen yet? I think Princess is going to have her baby today. Looks real close." Daddy sounded happy.

I peered at Princess. She looked scared. Her big brown eyes were really wide open and she was breathing funny. I knew something was about to happen.

Having seen other cows give birth, I quietly hoped that Princess wasn't ready yet. I never liked hearing her moan and grunt when the small hooves emerged.

"She's about to have it." Daddy began to unravel baler twine.

He tied the twine around my tummy and slid the other end snugly around the two small, pinkish-white hooves that were starting to emerge. Then he tied the twine around his own waist.

"OK. I think she's ready. Pull back when I say so ... OK, Pull back."

Pretty soon, I could see the calf's pink nose as it slid out onto the straw. I didn't know what the other stuff was that came out. I asked Daddy and he said it helped keep the baby safe when it was growing inside her mother. I didn't like looking at it and it smelled bad.

I was glad when he untied the twine around me. He told me that I could pat the baby's pretty black-and-white coat, which was wet, soft, and shiny.

In a few minutes, Princess began to lick her baby. I was happy to see that she loved her calf.

Cowpie Fights

One day, I heard my brother shouting something to my sister, about getting back at her. My sister yelled that she didn't care what he thought. I didn't know what they were fighting about. Then he leaned down, picked up something from the ground and ran toward her. I couldn't believe what I was seeing: he had scooped up a handful of a fresh cow pie and thrown it at her.

"Here, take this. You're not going to beat me up anymore." He threw another one before running into the barn, laughing. My sister started crying as she wiped the brown, smelly goo off her face and blouse. She stumbled toward the house.

I wondered what our parents were going to say at supper. Who was going to get yelled at? Probably my brother. Daddy was mean to him most of the time.

Angry Rats

Sissie's barking signaled that rats were close by in our barnyard as she feverishly dug dirt away from the top of a hole, sniffing, and waging her tail. Daddy had told me to stand close to the hole and hold the baseball bat tightly. He stood at the other end of the hole, pouring in water from the garden hose. I wondered why I had to stand at the hole where the angry, drowning rats appeared while Daddy just held the hose from some distance away.

He told me that when I saw the rats coming out of the hole, I was supposed to hit them with the bat. When they scurried out of the hole, they were soaking wet, their ears back, baring their teeth in their tiny triangle faces. I was scared that one was going to run up my leg because one had done that before. Most of the wet, angry rats ran off to the nearby corn crib, where a buffet of food awaited them.

Why, Daddy? Why?

I stared at my daddy standing by the electric fence as he licked a blade of grass like it was an ice cream cone.

Why is he putting grass in his mouth? I wondered. Only our cows ate grass.

"What are you doing, Daddy?"

He had just shut off our old Case tractor close to a nearby wire fence.

"Why are you doing that with the grass?" I asked again, curious.

"We have to test the electric fence to make sure it's working. The cows get a shock if they try to get out of the pasture. They don't like it because it tingles, so they stay away."

He licked a blade of grass and handed it to me.

"Here. Get up close." Then he told me to touch the wet blade to the wire while it was in my mouth.

My whole body shook. I was so scared.

He loves me. Why is he hurting me?

"Now our cows will stay home."

I never knew why he made me lick the grass. I never told my mother, either. I still don't know why I didn't.

Years later, I asked my brother if our father had ever made him test the fence.

"Christ, yes! I hated every time he handed me that wet grass. I wanted to hit him, but I knew if I tried, my punishment would be more severe than getting shocked. I got him back, though. I had only been home from school a few weeks when he said he needed help with a chore behind the barn. Before long, he took a swing, but I smacked him so hard he fell to the ground. He never laid a hand on me again."

"Good for you. I hated testing the fence too."

Robert looked surprised. "He made you test the fence too? No way. You were so young! Besides, you were always his favorite."

"Yes, I was around six when he started making me do it. It was like he was never concerned about how scary and hurtful it was."

Galileo and Copernicus

My favorite "curbside cuties" were two ducks named Galileo and Copernicus, names my Aunt Evie had given them. A family from church couldn't keep them as the kids had gone off to college, so we took them. I liked those ducks right away. Every morning when I walked from our house to the barn, they waddled around near the toolshed where they slept at night.

One morning, several months after they arrived, I couldn't believe my eyes. On top of a fence post were their chopped-off heads. I ran into the house, crying.

"Mommy, you knew I loved them. Poor things. Why didn't you stop him?"

"I'm sorry, Sweetie. I didn't know he was going to do this."

"Don't you dare put them in a cooking pot. Let's go, Sissie!" Tears continued to stream down my face as I ran out into the field behind the barn.

Dangers Abound on the Farm

Farming is Not for the Faint-Hearted

I had dodged a bullet, been kicked in the head by one of our cows, fallen off Lucky, and had a fresh cowpie tossed in my face. But my brother, sister, and I never had any bad accidents working on the farm. Our family was unique among the local farmers— neighbor kids and parents lost arms, fingers, and parts of feet in the greasy moving parts of hay balers and combines. Hands were crushed and mangled hooking up wagons behind tractors.

Three years old and already an animal lover.

I did, though, lose two dogs that were run over by the school bus. Also our bulldog, Mike, was hit by a stray arrow during hunting season. I kept a watchful eye on my beloved Sissie.

When I was four years old, I managed to step aside as a ten-year-old cousin pulled the trigger on a 12-gauge shotgun. His shot left a two-inch hole in the cement floor of our back porch. For whatever reason, I had moved out of his range a minute before he pulled the trigger.

I was seven when I was thrown off Lucky as he galloped down our driveway past the kitchen window, sending my mother chasing in wild pursuit.

Some years later, I was kicked in the head by an angry 2,000-pound Holstein cow, which left streams of blood flowing down my face. Unfortunately, I was standing behind the cow rather than on her side. All it took was one swift kick backwards. Lesson learned!

Those Scary Hills

One day during haying season, when I was around twelve, my father hooked up the baler and wagon to the back of our tractor. The baler bundled the alfalfa into fifty-pound bales that were then stacked on the wagon. I was driving the tractor. I didn't mind pulling the baler and wagon on the flat fields, but I was scared when I had to pull them up steep hills. I wondered if the tractor was strong enough. It turned out that my fears came true; the front of the tractor began to lift off the ground. I froze, clutching the steering wheel.

My father yelled, but I couldn't hear him above the noise of the baler until he got closer. It seemed forever before he was near enough to tell me to slowly let the tractor roll backward. I followed his orders. I was shaking, but relieved, when the front wheel slowly touched the ground. My father accepted my pleas not to have to steer on the hills again.

Doing chores.

Cows coming home to be milked.

I took good care of my baby calf.

A Hard Life

Farming life back in the 1950s was full of challenges, especially for small farmers who didn't have modern equipment and often relied on unpredictable weather reports. There were never any guarantees. Unforeseen events, such as heavy rains, fierce winds, or driving hail destroyed crops. Of course, there were also the dreaded tornados.

Looking back, I think that only God could have gotten my father to quit baling hay before a storm. Storms were soul-destroying. The eighteen years I spent growing up on our farm

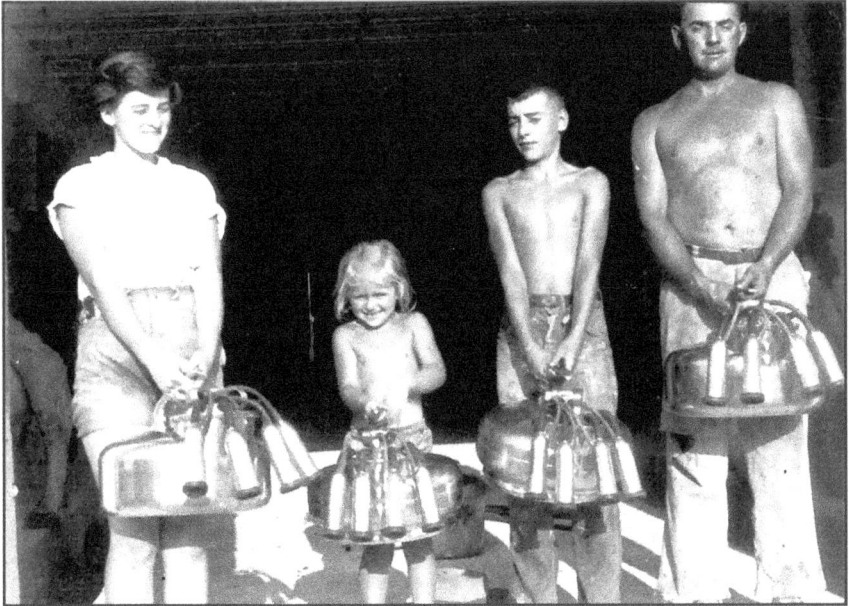

The Winns holding the milking machines.

made me realize that farmers needed strong bodies and big doses of optimism.

Mother Nature—A Force on the Farm

Daddy rushed through the screen door at the back of the house and yelled, "A storm's on its way. Come help." Then he rushed out again, slamming the door before heading to the barn. Mommy took off her apron and wiped her hands quickly.

She took my hand as we hurried toward the barn. With their heads down, Lucky and Vicki walked to a nearby shed. The cows huddled together along one of the barn walls.

Sissie hurried alongside Mommy and me, her tail down. She must have known that something was wrong. I think she was scared.

Daddy yelled again.

"Close all the doors. Lock them. Hurry!"

Mommy, Sissie, and I then ran back to the house. No leaves moved as we passed our two tall oak trees. The sky was covered with a soupy green blanket, like the color of the lima beans I hated.

We all huddled together on an old ratty sofa in the far corner of the basement.

Daddy said that we had to be in the corner in the direction the tornado was coming. I didn't know why, but wasn't going to ask right then. I might get more scared. We could hear the roar of the winds getting louder as the sky turned black. Daddy said that it looked like the tornado was coming from the direction of our town.

Mommy had her arm around me and told me that we were in the basement so we would be safe.

"What about Lucky and Vicki?" I started crying.

"Yes, they went into their shed just like we are doing here."

Suddenly, we heard a big whooshing sound and a roar like the wolf in the recording of *Peter and the Wolf* on my little plastic record player. We sat in the basement for what seemed like a very long time. The wind blew really hard. Then it was quiet and very scary.

We were lucky, but our neighbors weren't so fortunate. The tornado had destroyed two barns and a house, turned two Case tractors upside down, and killed a number of Holsteins.

Daddy checked on our cows, as well as our horses. They were all safe.

SHOWTIME AT THE STATE FAIR

It was showtime for me and my prom partner Princess, who had grown into a beautiful two-ton Holstein cow. She and I entered a noisy, vast show ring at the Wisconsin State Fair, along with twenty other competitors.

My father, mother, and I were putting the finishing touches on Princess to make her look her best before she entered the competition at the Wisconsin State Fair. She stood still as I rubbed baby powder onto her front legs to hide the yellow stains. My mother brushed the coarse switch at the end of Princess's tail, turning it into what looked like a wide, white, fluffy fan. This fussing over Princess reminded me of my mother getting Diane ready as she prepped for her high school prom.

We were grooming Princess in a drafty structure that housed the contestants. My father sat on a bale of hay, mixing beet pulp, water, and six bottles of Pabst Blue Ribbon beer in a metal bucket. Princess slurped the mixture with gusto. There was plenty of time for the carbonated mixture to round out her tummy perfectly. My father had also milked her an hour earlier, so her udder filled out just right; her full teats hung straight.

I slipped Princess' shiny black leather halter over her head and double-checked that it fit snuggly. We headed for the ring.

"Good luck, Sweetie," my mother said. She looked worried as she and my father walked away to find a seat in the arena.

Maybe she was remembering what had happened to me just two weeks earlier at the Walworth County Fair. Princess

had suddenly jumped on the cow in front of her and then dragged me along the sawdust floor. I had caught sight of my father, who was standing along the wall on the other side of the ring, thirty feet away. I had hoped he could help me get control of Princess, but his arms were crossed. He just stared, but didn't come to my rescue. Mother told me after we got home that she wished that my father had helped. A nice man leading his cow behind me yanked Princess's halter a few times and made sure that I had a good grip on her again.

My hands were still tender. It hadn't been Princess's fault; she had just come into heat. I was 12 years old and didn't exactly know why that happened or what it meant. However, when cows are in heat, they act up and get weird. I was hoping that Princess would behave this time.

The Show Begins

Princess and I began to amble along the path toward the arena. I soon realized that the path was covered with smelly, fresh cowpies. I dodged them as well as I could, but suddenly felt warm, brown poop soak into my white Converse shoes. I just hoped that no one else would notice my embarrassing situation.

A loudspeaker announced that the two-year-old Holstein open class competition was about to begin. These competitions allowed large, well-known breeders to compete along with small farmers and 4-H Club kids like me. Usually, the large breeders won in this competition.

Princess wasn't scared by the noise so far, which was a good sign. I had spent months training her to walk slowly and respond to the tug of her halter. Even with the training, there were no guarantees of what might happen once she and the other cows entered the ring. Often, one or two became unruly because they hadn't been trained well. Others were in heat, or

Showing Princess at the Wisconsin State Fair.

maybe they were just spooked by the constant and unfamiliar noise in the arena.

"Okay, here we go," I whispered to my pretty black-and-white bovine. My head was just about even with her strong shoulders. Princess was perfectly relaxed, chewing her cud as we slowly trudged along the perimeter of the arena. I tugged on her halter in an effort to stop her from chewing. Usually, when a cow chews her cud, she's content. She may even be digesting her latest meal. However, in the show ring, judges like to see a more alert animal.

After stepping into the ring, I slowly began walking backwards, facing Princess. The caravan of competitors began to follow one another along the perimeter of the ring—person, cow, person, cow—plodding one after another.

Princess was walking perfectly, chewing her cud. I gave her halter a quick, hard tug when I saw the judge coming our way. He circled around us several times before moving on to look at the other cows.

"Keep it up," I whispered. "Good girl."

Just then, she lifted her tail and pooped. *Plop. Plop. Plop.* Thank goodness, the judge wasn't nearby any longer.

Must be that beet pulp!

After looking at all the cows, the judge beckoned me and an older breeder to move our animals into the blue-ribbon line, where we joined three others. Soon, he nodded to the older breeder to move his animal into first place in the blue-ribbon line, leaving me in second.

I wasn't happy; I thought Princess was definitely a better-looking cow. Then again, I told myself, he must be some well-known, big-time breeder. I figured that Princess and I didn't have a chance since we were from a small farm.

Just as I loosened my grip, the judge came back and motioned Princess and me to step out of the line where the other contestants were continuing to lead their cows. He circled around Princess and patted her on her shoulder. My knees were shaky, but Princess was perfectly calm. She was not chewing her cud. The judge slowly looked her up and down before assessing the other cow to determine which one would be champion. He beckoned Princess and me to the front of the blue-ribbon line.

"Congratulations! Good work, young gal," he said, smiling broadly. "She's a beautiful animal. And you trained her well."

"We won, Princess!" I said softly, giving her a hug. I was relieved that I hadn't gotten dragged around again and happy the show was over.

I wondered if my father was pleased by the win. I think he had a faint smile on his face, but I couldn't really tell. Maybe it was the distance.

I spotted my mother, grinning broadly. She was taking a picture with our old Kodak camera that pulled out like an accordion.

Suddenly, I heard over a loudspeaker, "Miss Kay Winn from the Whitewater 4-H Club and Princess are winners in this two-year-old class." *We won!*

People clapped. Princess burped, leaving a gob of pink saliva on my arm. Alice in Dairyland, the 4-H version of Miss Wisconsin, stood next to us and smiled as she patted Princess' neck.

"Congratulations! You two did a good job today. You should be very happy."

As the pretty blond Alice was handing me the blue ribbon, Princess belched again. A flood of yucky beet pulp streamed out of her mouth and landed on the pastel-blue skirt of Alice's polka-dot dress. I yanked on Princess's halter, but I knew she couldn't help herself. Maybe she just had to let go of that nasty beet pulp.

"I'm sorry. So sorry," I tried very hard to hold back tears. Alice in Dairyland wiped what she could off her dress as she

Three junior exhibitors from the Whitewater 4-H club had an enviable record at the at the Walworth County fairgrounds Friday. The three showed seven animals, winning a blue on each. Shown counting their ribbons are (from left) Bob Winn and his junior heifer calf, Kay Winn looking at camera) and Becky Mason. (*Whitewater Register*)

My friend Becky and me with our prize-winning cows.

gingerly attempted to smile at the crowd as she made her way out of the arena.

A nice man offered Alice a handkerchief. As it turned out, he was indeed a big-time breeder. He patted Princess on her shoulder and smiled.

"Don't be upset. These things happen with our cows. You know, if I were the judge here today, I would have chosen you as number one too. Good work."

I was still trying to hold back tears as I led Princess toward my mother and father. I handed the trophy to my mother. My father took Princess's halter and headed back to her stall, where she would sleep until we headed home in the morning.

"Beautiful animal," someone yelled. My father nodded and lifted his grubby, sweat-stained Burpee Seed cap.

"I'm so sad. It's terrible what happened," I blurted to my mother.

"You couldn't help it. I'm so proud of you. Daddy is too." She gave me a hug. My father didn't say anything, but a slight grin appeared on his face. Mother and I walked behind him.

I looked down at the blue ribbon clasped in my sweaty hand. I was so glad the show was over, at least for another year.

FUN TIMES ON THE FARM

I remember riding in the front seat of my sister's new 1958 baby-blue and white Chevy Impala convertible as we drove along Main Street. I had never been in a convertible before. The top was down and the warm wind felt nice blowing on my face. My sister assured me as she drove out of our driveway and onto the highway to town that I wouldn't fly off my seat into the open sky. After I started feeling safe in the car, I enjoyed the ride. I loved the colors of the car and the smooth feel of the seat. I wondered how the radio could work when we were in the car and not at home.

Was this how the people in town who lived in the nice, big houses and drove fancy cars felt? Convertibles were rare, so a few people stared, stopping on the sidewalk as we passed. Bob from Bob's Shoe Store waved and smiled. Some others waved too. I hoped that we would see one of my big-house friends so I could show off, even a little.

Serenading the Music Lovers

When I was older, for special fun, sometimes I walked along Reliance Road from our barn to the white wooden fence surrounding the pasture where our cows were resting and chewing their cuds.

I don't know why I decided to play my second-hand alto saxophone for them, but I nevertheless stood close to the fence, blaring out different notes very poorly. (My mother had purchased the used sax for me.) I didn't know any songs, but that clearly didn't matter to the cows. It wasn't long before several of them trotted toward me at a good pace. They had just been milked a short time earlier, so their udders were really swinging side to side as they approached the fence.

Before long, more wandered close by. Some snorted and pressed their wet noses through the fence. Even the older cows managed to get up from their snoozes to come join in the concert. All eyes were on me. Music lovers all!

Sometimes I laughed and patted those who ventured closest.

Years later, I learned that soothing music has a calming effect on cows and can increase milk production. One study, *The Surprising Internal and Social Life of Cows* (Ann Jones) found that a popular song was "Bridge Over Troubled Water" by Simon & Garfunkel. "Moon River," sung by Andy Williams, was another popular tune. Maybe classical music might have such an impact, but it's doubtful that my poor performance encouraged increased milk production.

I also learned that cows are smart. I should have known that as I was always amazed that our cows knew which stanchions were theirs when they entered the barn to be milked twice a day. One by one, they would step over the gutters and walk into their respective places.

The Winn family (L to R): Robert, Diane, me holding my daddy's hand, my mother, my father.

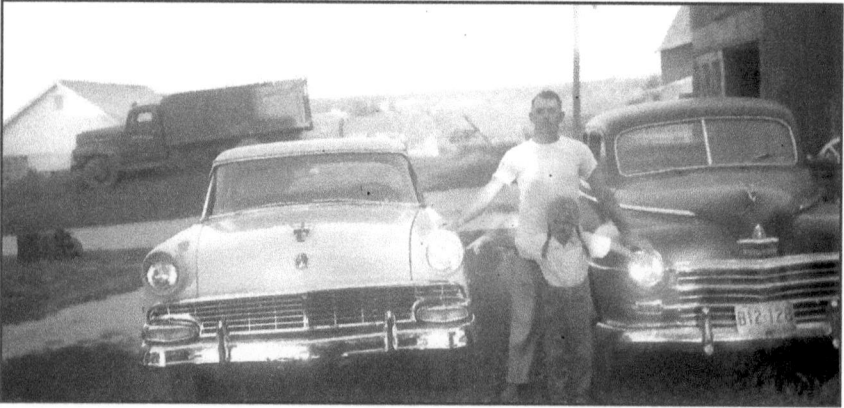

Daddy and me getting ready to go into town.

Friday Nights in Whitewater

Sometimes, when our cows were milked and none were expected to deliver a calf, my father drove us to the local A&W Root Beer stand on the edge of town. He would park in one of the small stalls separated by posts with attached menus. We called in our orders on a speaker phone.

My father always ordered a large root beer float that cost 99 cents. My brother usually ordered a hot dog for 99 cents. My mother, sister, and I ordered the regular root beer in a frosted mug, which was 89 cents. I liked to lick the frost off the mug, especially after spending a day in the hot July sun.

My sister worked as a carhop at the drive-in for a few months. She hopped from car to car delivering orders. Specially designed car trays were clipped to our window, which had to be rolled up a few inches to accommodate the food. When we were done with our treats, the protocol was to turn on the headlights to signal the carhop to retrieve the trays and mugs.

High School, College, Career

Bascom Hill, University of Wisconsin–Madison, site of some of the anti-war protests in the 1960s and 1970s.

RIP—JOHN F. KENNEDY
NOVEMBER 22, 1963

*"It ought to be possible, in short, for every American
to enjoy the privileges of being American
without regard to his race or his color."*

I had just read this quote from President Kennedy as I
wrapped up my final side of a debate about civil rights in
my freshman high school civics class. I had quoted him often
as I defended his positions supporting civil rights. Suddenly, I
was startled by the abrupt crackle from our school loud
speaker.

Tap. Tap. Tap.

Silence, then *Tap. Tap. Tap* again.

"Hello. Hello. This is your principal speaking. Please may
I have your attention. I have very sad news. It has just been
reported that President Kennedy has been shot while riding
in a presidential motorcade in Dallas, Texas. He's been taken
to a nearby hospital. That's all we know now, but we should
hear more about his condition soon. I ask that everyone please
proceed to the gym."

I suddenly started to giggle, uncontrollably, but covered
my mouth hoping that no one noticed. I don't know why that
happened when we had just heard such awful news. It must
have been a bad case of the nerves, but it was a weird reaction. Maybe I was in shock. I was only twelve, but I was in
awe of our president.

My parents were proud Democrats and liked our president. They believed in what President Kennedy stood for. I

made a scrapbook cutting out newspaper clippings about him and his family.

I remembered an invitation that then-Senator Kennedy sent to my parents inviting them to a breakfast in Madison. I was proud that they received it, especially since my father was just a small dairy farmer and my mother was a teacher. I had the invitation framed, as well as a letter from the senator dated January 9, 1960. He wrote that the challenges of the 1960s demanded new ideas, new action, and the need to offer voters constructive new solutions.

* * *

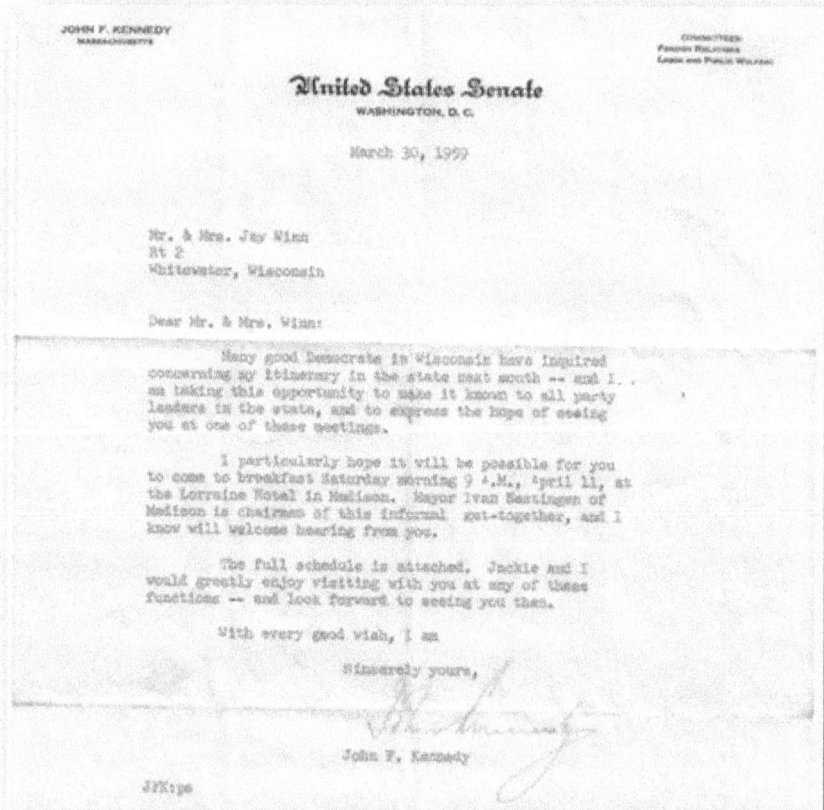

Breakfast invitation from Senator J. F. Kennedy

Our teacher took out his handkerchief and wiped away tears from behind his black glasses as he paced back and forth on his short legs, twisting his pencil in his hand.

"Let's get going, everyone."

Larry, my debate partner, and I, and the other twelve students in our class all rose slowly from our desks and shuffled out in orderly columns. Larry had a deer-in-the-headlights look.

Everyone was dazed; nobody goofed around or broke ranks to talk. It was sobering to see the usually loud kids standing in silence with their heads bowed.

Fluorescent lights hummed overhead amid the muffled cries and coughs. The boys who had been playing basketball for gym class briefly held their basketballs close to their chests before putting them down, the uncollected balls lying at their feet.

My friend Shirley whispered as she tugged at her upper lip, "What are we going to do if he dies? We have no president and the Russians will come! There'll be a war. Oh, my God ..." She began to cry, twisting her ponytail round and round in her hand. I did wonder if the Russians would bomb us now. I quietly wished I could be with my mother in her classroom just down the hall.

One of the Whitewater Whippets cheerleaders, Linda, had a red, puffy face as she turned to me and whispered, "This is so scary. Aren't you scared?" She began to whimper.

"Of course, I am, but I don't want to talk about it right now, okay?"

I looked around, but everywhere it was the same: girls crying, boys shifting from foot to foot. The stale odor wafting from the boys' locker room, coupled with the hot air that had permeated the gym, made me feel like throwing up.

Finally, our principal emerged and stood up on a bleacher to address us. "I'm sorry to announce that our president has died. Mrs. Kennedy was with him in the motorcade, but she was not injured. I want you all to know that our country will be safe. We are a strong country and we will survive this terrible, terrible tragedy. Vice President Johnson will be sworn in as our 36th president soon.

"How thankful we should be that our Constitution makes the transfer of power so peaceful. It is foresighted and clearly timeless. President Kennedy was a great man—a shining example of what we all should aspire to: a friend of the poor and a crusader against the Communists and other adversaries across the ocean. Let us pray for the First Lady and Vice President Johnson, and for our country."

I don't remember exactly what else he said, but his words made me feel a little better. He wrapped up saying that school would be closed for the rest of the day; the football game scheduled for that night was cancelled.

I walked over to the junior high to where my mother was packing up after another day of teaching.

"Did you hear? He died. Our president. It's scary, isn't it? And so sad."

"Yes, it was announced over the loud speaker. It's terrible news." She seemed distracted as she gathered student papers to take home to grade. Maybe she had had a stressful day of teaching or she was grieving and overwhelmed by the awful news—or both.

Silence filled the car as she drove us back to our farm. Although I wanted to hear more about what happened, I didn't ask her to turn on the radio. After we arrived home and she shut off the car's engine, she turned to me. She was teary-eyed and reached for my hand.

"Sweetie, our country is strong. We will get through these dark and unpredictable days. Let's hope that our new president and his advisors will make the right decisions.

"I just can't imagine who would want to kill our president; it's such a horrible act of violence, so awful for the First Lady and the rest of the Kennedy family. Hopefully, Mr. Cronkite in his newscast tonight will add clarity to today's awful events and offer all television viewers some reassurance and comfort."

MORNING DRIVES TO HIGH SCHOOL WITH MY PROGRESSIVE MOTHER

Mother and I spent many mornings together when she drove me to high school before heading to teach. We listened to music or to a public radio station that talked about major issues of the times: the Civil Rights movement, the Vietnam war, the battle for equal rights.

I thought she was amazing, so progressive for her generation, especially in Whitewater, a small, conservative, Republican town. She drove 55 miles per hour to get the best gas mileage and to help reduce pollution. She supported the Equal Rights Amendment, which stated "Equality of rights under the law shall not be denied or abridged by the United States or by any state on account of sex." Most of her Republican friends opposed it. Later, when their daughters were looking for jobs, those same friends called "Foul." Too many males were getting chosen over the girls. As a true Midwesterner, my mother didn't gloat.

The Issue of Race

One morning, there was a discussion on the radio about the plight of black people. The words just rolled off her tongue: "If they really want to help the Blacks, they should educate them."

I was sixteen and very impressed that she was so wise without having had a mother from whom to learn and ask questions.

Some buttons from those early days:
- ERA in support of the Equal Rights Amendment;
- Carter/Mondale / Jimmy and Fritz running for president and vice president;
- Crossed-through hanger to represent the Pro-Choice movement.

Franklin Junior High School where my mother taught home economics.

My mother made me so proud.

IT'S COMPLICATED

I was proud to tell my high school friends that I had only heard my father yell at my mother twice. There were words exchanged in hushed tones, but I never really understood what was being said. My girlfriends told me stories about their parents yelling at each other or about a mother who had a drinking problem. I felt so sad for them.

Even though I don't remember my parents ever shouting, I knew that we all had to be toiling away at something to keep my father happy. He was demanding and had a quick temper, so we tiptoed around him. My mother and sister always babied and fawned over him. It was hard to digest. My resentfulness grew as I quietly watched how he treated our family.

He welcomed any scant attention I gave him, especially since I was his favorite. Even so, I still resented him. I was particularly upset by how he treated my mother after all she did for him. Yet, just as upsetting was the fact that she let him. I struggled with how to reconcile my vision of her with who she actually was around him. I couldn't square all of the wisdom she instilled, the strength she demonstrated, and the love she gave me, with her submissiveness and absolute devotion to him.

Maybe she was, well, human. Fallible?

Raymond "Buddie" Robinson–Whitewater Warrior (1968)

"I have bad news. Buddie Robinson was killed in the fighting. Don't know when it happened. Vietnam is far away. No one knows much." My father cleared his throat and dug into the mashed potatoes and roast beef my mother had prepared for lunch.

"What? Buddie's dead? How did you find out?" I was stunned.

"Heard it at the co-op. They were saying what a good athlete he was. All-around nice guy."

My best friend from high school was dead. Unbelievable. Why him?

I was numb, trying to absorb my father's words. As I began to weep, my mother rose from her chair and hugged me.

"So sorry, Sweetie. I know he meant a lot to you; he was special to all of us. " She struggled to speak.

Too upset to eat, I followed my father back out to the fields. Rain was predicted, so he was in a rush to get the alfalfa cut. I climbed up on our old Case tractor and began the tedious task of driving back and forth across the field. Not only was the work boring, but it was ninety degrees and humid. The sweat stung my eyes.

Alone now, in my own world, I thought about Buddie. I loved his big heart, his gentle nature, and crooked smile. Anger. Sadness. So many emotions and questions:

How did he die? Did he suffer? When will his body be sent home? Was this war worth all the young boys coming home in body bags?

73

College felt like a distant past, even though I had only been home for three weeks for summer break. Madison seemed so far away.

The days were predictable: milking and feeding the cows, scooping up and spreading manure, baling hay, and painting fences. The nights were filled with the distant barks of neighbors' dogs and the muffled sounds of semis traveling on the highway a mile away.

It was no wonder that I couldn't wait to leave the farm after graduation and head to Madison!

As was true of many small towns, Whitewater was proud of its athletes. Our teams defined us; they were the center of gravity. One of Whitewater's best all-around athletes was Buddie, who had won letters in football, wrestling, and track.

Friday nights, farmers, bankers, parents of the athletes, and other local townsfolk climbed up the wooden bleachers to cheer for Buddie and the Whitewater Whippets football team. Floodlights cast a round, yellow glow over the football field, as though a giant flashlight were being held in the sky. Whistles of the referees, grunts of the boys tackling each other, and cheers from the bleachers pierced the evening air.

"Go, Buddie! Go!" I would shout as he scrambled down the field. He was the go-to guy when the team really needed to score.

After one game, he awkwardly asked me if I wanted to wear his letter jacket. (Letter jackets were worn by athletes who excelled in a sport.) I gained new confidence wearing it and holding his warm hand: I was more than just "a farm girl." My city friends wore nice clothes and always strolled down the hall looking so cool. I really didn't know what *it* was, but I knew I didn't have *it*.

* * *

After high school graduation, Buddie joined the Navy; I headed to the University of Wisconsin (UW) in Madison. The parents of some of my friends thought that the UW campus was infested with pampered anarchists, hippies, and other anti-war radicals—a place to be avoided at all costs. They believed that some things that happened in Madison were too awful to talk about.

Within weeks after classes started in October 1967, a violent police riot broke out on campus. Students rushed past my political science classroom windows like an invading army. Riot-squad policemen armed with Billy clubs were chasing them down Bascom Hill, clubbing those in their path and spraying them with tear gas. Kids were holding up signs and shouting *"Hey, hey, LBJ! How many kids did you kill today? Hey, hey, LBJ! How many kids did you kill today?"*

I ran in the opposite direction of the crowd and headed toward my dorm, but not before I too was a victim of the pepper gas. My eyes stung. Seeing protesters getting tackled and clubbed to the ground terrified me. I felt alone and scared.

I squinted at a sign attached to a piece of wood trampled on the street. It read, "Get out, Dow."

What in the world does that mean?

Back in the lobby of my dorm, I asked Rona, who lived two rooms away from mine, "What's going on? I mean, who is Dow, anyway?"

"What? Dow? You don't know what Dow is?" Rona's voice rose. "They kill people, for crying out loud! They make napalm—the flammable gel stuff that's killing innocent children and villagers. Can you believe how stupid they are, coming here to Madison to recruit? I mean, tell me they're not fucking STUPID! And those Goddamned cops, splitting heads open with their fucking Billy clubs!"

Rona took a deep breath and stared at me, than blurted out, "Your eyes! You got gassed. Hurry! Get a cloth and put cold water on them. Don't rub them, though. I'm heading out." Rona raised her fist and her poster in defiance.

I squinted, trying to make out the words. Rona shouted, "Get it? You probably can't read it with your eyes messed up. It says, 'Bombing for peace is like fucking for virginity!' And she stormed out the door.

"I got it," I replied sheepishly.

She'll be out there in the middle of the melee holding that sign. That takes guts!

During those early riots, police cars were stoned. Fires were set in garbage dumpsters and then shoved into the streets. Students screamed at TVs when President Johnson or Secretary of Defense Robert McNamara repeatedly told Americans that our troops were winning the war, that casualties were declining, and that more troops would be returning home soon. CBS News anchor Walter Cronkite—"the most trusted man in America" at that time— with his steady voice, dutifully relayed administration updates from reporters in the war zone.

The protestors accused the President and other government leaders of lying to the American people. They questioned why young men were being sent into battles to be slaughtered. More Americans began to question our involvement in Vietnam as casualties began to mount. The protesters' voices grew louder; body bags were dragged in front of TV viewers. Newspapers around the country increased their coverage. The UW-Madison's student demonstrations were some of the first in the U.S. to turn violent—presaging the coming months of the bloody consequences of national turmoil.

* * *

"Our President, lying to the American public? No way," I told myself.

I felt ashamed and stupid. I even had to look up where Vietnam was on a map. We didn't talk about the war much on the farm, even though my brother was in the Army. My parents were proud that he was serving his country and was a member of the elite Army's Fife and Drum Corps. They believed that the U.S. was engaged in Vietnam for good reasons. After all, that's what we were told. For much longer than I wanted to admit, I quietly clung to their view.

* * *

As protesters' voices grew more impassioned, they marched on Bascom Hill, and I felt compelled to join them. I was majoring in journalism so I wanted to witness firsthand what was happening. I smelled the pepper gas, saw the bloodied heads, and heard the screams of rage.

* * *

A Sad Day

Even at 7:30 that July morning, I could tell it was going to be a steamy day for Buddie's funeral. The cows lumbered out of the barn more slowly than usual, their tails swishing from side to side, brushing away flies.

I dreaded this day. *How sad will it be seeing Buddie's family? Will I keep it together? Will the small church hold all the people paying their respects?*

As a student, I lived in my bell bottoms and didn't own a black dress. So, I slipped on a plain blue cotton one.

"Are you ready?" my mother yelled. "We have to get going. Your father's waiting."

God, what else is new? Always the first one in that damned car waiting for us. Honking!

Mother had made Danish orange rolls and a rhubarb pie to give to Buddie's family. Even with the windows down, the sweet aromas quickly filled our hot car. It was a smell I usually loved, but today, it made me nauseous.

My father glanced at the neighbors' crops along the way, as he always did. Sometimes my mother would say how good Mr. Millard's corn looked. My father hated it when the neighbors' corn was higher than ours or when they had finished baling a crop of hay before us. Even in my early teens, I recognized that my father was an insecure, jealous man.

As we walked into the church, the bank president, who also owned a dairy supply company, nodded to my parents. I glanced around and was shocked to see so few teachers, high school administrators, or coaches there. Scattered though the pews was a handful of folks from around town, a few farmers who lived near the Robinsons, a couple of local businessmen, and some Whitewater Whippet sports boosters. The low turn-out infuriated me.

Reverend Engel talked about things we must accept that we don't understand. He stressed that Buddie had died honorably fighting for our country. He spoke of Buddie's contributions to Whitewater sports and how he had made the community so proud. Buddie's younger brother read a letter the family had received two days before they were notified of his death. He shared Buddie's longing to get back home and his hope that the war would end soon before more boys got killed.

> *"Too many guys are dying. This place is a mess.*
> *Can't wait to get back."*

We recited the Twenty-Third Psalm.

* * *

On the drive back to our farm, my mother spoke up.

"That was a lovely service. He was so young. It's so hard on the family." Her voice trailed off; I thought she was trying not to cry.

* * *

My Sleepless Night

That night was the first time in my life I couldn't sleep. I was angry and confused. I sat up in bed and began writing.

The next morning at breakfast, I told my parents that I had written a letter and wanted to take it to the local newspaper office to be printed.

"It makes me sick. They showed no respect for Buddie or his family." I stared at my plate of pancakes.

"You go ahead," my mother declared. "I understand that you're angry and let down. I have always encouraged you to do what you think is right. Now is one of these times."

"Well, I don't know. Let's think about this," my father interjected.

"Maybe things came up for them. We don't know … Just because some didn't go to the funeral, doesn't mean that they didn't care," he chimed in after swallowing the last bits of his scrambled eggs. He blew his nose in his ratty handkerchief.

His comment shocked me; he rarely had much to say. I was so taken aback that I almost choked on my toast.

"Dad, really? Weren't you embarrassed by the low turn-out? You really liked Buddie."

My mother frowned, staring at him as she slowly stirred her black coffee.

"Well, Kay, you should be careful," Dad said. You have to keep in mind that your mother is a teacher. If your letter is printed, some folks might want to cause problems. This is a small town. I'm just saying, think about this a little more before you do anything."

"Of course, I don't want to act in any way that could cause problems for my mom. She has a good reputation with her colleagues. She said 'Now's the time.' Right, Mother?"

"Yes, Sweetie. Now's the time," she responded.

My father grabbed his grubby cap and headed to the barn. I sensed that he had more to say, but decided it was best to leave before I got angrier.

* * *

Taking Action

"Hello, sir. I am Kay Winn." I was about to tell the owner and editor of the paper why I was there when he interrupted.

"A Winn girl, are you? Leonard's daughter?"

"No, my father is Jay."

"The farmer out on Reliance Road? Your mother's a teacher, is that right?"

"Yes, that's right. I'm here because I have a Letter to the Editor to be printed."

"Sure. Let's take a look." He glanced at it quickly. "Here at the paper, we only print Letters to the Editor if they are signed. That's our policy."

He told me I would have to sign the letter in order to have it printed in the paper.

He said, "If someone wants to express his or her view about an issue—and felt strongly about it—they should be willing and even want to have their name printed too.

He handed me back my letter.

I felt my anger building. My hands were shaking. I could feel my face getting hotter and sweat spreading under my arms.

"Sir, Buddie died for our country. He died trying to make the world a better place. At least that's what our leaders are telling us all, right? To make us safer. You know that, right? You can't hide from the war. Buddie made Whitewater proud, didn't he?"

He peered down at me. "I'm sorry."

Again, insincerity.

Hopping Mad!

I took my anger and headed home. Further words would be wasted on him. *What a ridiculous policy.* I shouldn't have been surprised. He and most of the locals were Republican; my parents were some of the few Democrats in the area.

The war had bled its way to Whitewater. I wondered if the "policy" would have been different if Buddie had been a young man from a rich family? Or if my parents weren't Democrats?

"So, how'd it go, Sweetie?" my mother asked when I walked into the kitchen.

"Well, he said that Letters to the Editor wouldn't be printed unless they're signed. Mother, he was so condescending. I'm am so bummed. So angry."

"Don't worry about me, Sweetie. You do what's right," she said.

"I know you haven't asked to see what I have written, but let me read it. I want to make sure readers hear my words and understand what has upset me so much."

She and my father put down their forks, having just finished lunch. Mother turned down the *Farm Report* on the radio.

She continued. "Sweetie, as I've told you before, do what you believe is right. That's the only way to live. I am proud of you for taking a stand. I was ashamed at the turnout, too. Maybe you'll wake up some people. That's all there's to it. Sign and deliver the letter."

My father nodded. "I've been thinking. You're right. Buddie deserved better."

No one from town ever said a word about the letter to me or my parents. Buddie Robinson was the first, but not the last, boy from Whitewater to come back home in a body bag.

LETTER DEPARTMENT

Whitewater Register Whitewater, Wisconsin

Dear Editor:

Each day many communities throughout the United States are unpleasantly reminded of the present war in Vietnam by the deaths of one or more of their area servicemen. With the recent tragic death of Raymond Robinson, Whitewater is reminded of the painful proximity of the war.

Raymond Robinson gave himself to his and our country to aid in the cause for peace. Raymond-Buddie, as he was so often called-not only represented the United States Navy, but also Whitewater, Wisconsin.

Buddie gave much of his time and talent to Whitewater High School. He had been president of his senior high school class, an All-Conference football player, wrestling captain, and a conference wrestling champion in his weight division. Because of his perseverence and competence, Buddie was able to attain these honors. Many Whitewater High School students, faculty members, and coaches were proud of what Buddie had contributed to Whitewater High School. We all shared in the honor that he brought to our school.

Since Buddie had contributed so much to Whitewater High School and our country, does it not seem logical that classmates, friends, and faculty members could have at least shown their respect by attending his service[1] Many of Buddie's classmates, teammates, and friends were at the service; however, the number of representatives of the Whitewater high school faculty, whether there were administrators, teachers, or coaches was very, very scant.

It seems very sad and disgusting that more of these representatives could not have given up a small portion of one day of their lives in respect to Raymond Robinson. It makes one wonder just how much one must do. It seems as though this time, these representatives could have given a little more time than just what they give in administering, teaching, and directing sports events for this young twenty year old graduate of Whitewater high school. He gave his life; what more could he give[1]   A member of the Whitewater
                                          High School Class of 1967
                                          Kay Winn

Taps

There will be a great encampment
In the land of clouds today.
A mingling and a merging
Of our boys who've gone away.
Though on earth they are disbanding,
They are very close and near,
For these brave and honored heroes
Show no sorrow, shed no tear.
They have lived a life of glory,
History pins their medals high,
Listen to the thunder rolling,
They are marching in the sky!

—ARTA NOTTINGHAM CHAPPIUS

IN MEMORY OF
Raymond D. Robinson

BORN
June 10, 1948
Edgerton, Wisconsin

PASSED AWAY
July 12, 1968
Vietnam

TIME AND PLACE OF SERVICES
1:00 p. m. Monday, July 29, 1968
Skindingsrude and Lein Funeral Home

CLERGYMAN
Rev. William Stevens
First Methodist Church
Kenosha, Wisconsin

INTERMENT
Greenridge Cemetery
Kenosha, Wisconsin

SKINDINGSRUDE & LEIN
Funeral Home

The Methodist Church in Whitewater, where Diane was
married and my parents had their funeral services.

ROBERT AND THE ARMY
FIFE AND DRUM CORPS

Taking a break from college in 1964, Robert joined the Old Guard Fife and Drum Corps, a premier musical organization of the U.S. Army. Members perform with fifes and wear uniforms like those used by military musicians of the Continental Army during the American Revolution.

The Corps participates in major pageants and historical celebrations throughout the U.S. and also performs for arrival ceremonies at the White House for foreign heads of state. The Corps has participated in every Presidential Inauguration Parade since President John F. Kennedy.

Robert had several years of piano experience and could read music, when the Corps was looking for new enrollees, Robert was chosen. According to his son, Blair, Robert liked serving in the Corps "from the way he talked about it."

So Close, So Far Away

It wasn't long after I moved to Madison to go to college that I realized that my relationship with my mother would never be the same as it had been when I was in high school.

For the first months, I felt overwhelmed coming from a town of approximately 5,000 residents, I was now surrounded by 32,000 other undergraduates.

We chatted on the phone once a week and she wrote me letters that helped me keep my fears and loneliness at bay.

Angry Mobs

When I was a student at UW–Madison between 1967 and 1971, it was difficult to escape the cloak of fear, confusion, and mistrust that the Vietnam War wrought.

The first student demonstration erupted as I sat in a freshman political science course. Suddenly, I heard voices yelling, bullhorns blaring, muffled words I couldn't understand. We all got up from our seats and looked out the window toward the top of Bascom Hill. I had no idea what was happening, just floods of other students wearing bandanas and yelling as they punched their clenched fists in the air. They were stampeding down the hill toward our building. The professor abruptly cancelled the class.

I quickly closed my notebook, followed others out the door, and headed up the hill. I scampered to the edge of the growing mass of faces and hurried to get away and across the campus to my dorm. I wanted to call my mother.

So Many Questions

True to my roots for better or worse, I read, questioned, and listened to my dorm mates and friends rant against President Johnson, the invasion of Cambodia, the Vietnam morass, and the draft. I think my parents clung to the idea that the President was trying to do his best. I held onto that same notion longer than I would like to admit.

However, I was quickly troubled and curious about the intensity of the students' passion, anger, and boldness. I hadn't experienced anything even remotely close to seeing thousands of people my age so filled with rage. They were willing to be clubbed by cops and dared to stare down National Guardsmen gripping rifles with sharp bayonets. I learned later that lots of the demonstrators were "out of state agitators," a term used almost daily by conservative state legislators. The ruckus made me realize that I had never been in contact with or met anyone who lived outside Wisconsin, other than relatives.

My First Newspaper Job — as a Volunteer

I joined the staff of *The Daily Cardinal*, the campus newspaper, a so-called "Communist rag," by those same lawmakers. I'm sure that some of my parents' friends quietly commented over numerous suppers that the Winn daughter was going to be corrupted by all the "hippies, commies, and far-left, out-of-state kids."

1970 SUMMER—
REPORTER FOR THE *MILWAUKEE COURIER*

The city already lay gasping like a big beast.

It was only 8:00 a.m., but the moist, oppressive air was steaming up my glasses. I was waiting for the bus at the 12th Street intersection, headed to Milwaukee's inner city.

For a minute, I wished I were back at the one-room apartment I was renting in a large colonial home on Lakeshore Drive, overlooking Lake Michigan. I could have basked in the cool, refreshing morning breezes blowing off the lake.

Two weeks earlier, I had begun a summer internship at the *Milwaukee Courier*, a Black-owned and -operated newspaper. I had just finished my junior year at the UW with a major in journalism, and was intent on finding a summer internship with a newspaper.

I usually timed it so I could hop from one bus to the other, but on this day, the second bus was late. I soon realized that I was the only White woman waiting. Several Black women were wiping their faces and fanning themselves. I smiled and said hello; some smiled back.

James Brown, a very popular soul singer, was blaring "I'm Black and I'm Proud" from a nearby bar's loudspeaker. A few people laughed as I jumped at the loud sound.

Such loud music at this hour? I liked soul, but this early in the morning?

Because the bus had always come on time, I hadn't noticed the bar until now. An elderly black woman, shabbily dressed and unsteady on her feet, stumbled out of the bar and tottered toward me. The other women quietly stared at her.

"Want to sell some pussy? Come on, Sugar Britches, sell some pussy. You got some sweet stuff there." The woman reached toward me, laughing.

"Leave her alone, you drunken bitch!" yelled one of the women waiting for the bus. This shut up the teetering woman, but not before she raised a middle finger and mumbled something about "fat ass." She turned and wandered off. Thankfully, the bus arrived and I quickly stepped onto it. Once I sat down, I realized that I was trembling.

Sugar Britches? Pussy? I never had heard those words before, but given how the woman said them and the way that she looked at me, it didn't take me long to figure out what she was suggesting.

I looked at the bus pass in my unsteady hand. June 14, 1970. It was already shaping up to be quite a summer! I thought back over the past month; nothing had gone as planned and that's why I was sitting on a dirty bus inhaling exhaust fumes in Wisconsin's largest metropolitan center.

* * *

My plans to intern for a U.S. senator had fallen apart at the last minute. The internship likely went to the son or daughter of a bigwig with political connections. My father was active in the local Democratic party, but was no match for the people with connections.

This setback fueled my mission to find work at a newspaper. I borrowed my parents' car and drove an hour and a half from the farm to Milwaukee. I located a phone booth where I began scanning the Yellow Pages, looking under "newspapers" and "publications."

My assumption that I was too late to apply for an internship with either of the two large Milwaukee newspapers, the *Milwaukee Journal* and the *Milwaukee Sentinel*, proved to be correct. However, I came across a listing for the *Milwaukee Courier*. After dialing the number, I heard a low, soft male voice. I said I was a journalism major at Madison looking for a summer internship.

"I was wondering if you have any summer job openings?"

"Really don't think so. I can check with the boss, though. Can you hold? First, just one question. Are you okay working for a Black newspaper? You know this is a Black newspaper..." his voice trailed off.

"No, I don't mind." I said timidly, clutching the phone. I actually hadn't realized it was a Black-owned newspaper, so I was taken aback. While he was checking with his boss, doubts began to percolate in my head.

Do I really want to do this?

I wiped the sweat from my forehead; I was burning up from the sun beating into the smelly, cramped phone booth.

"Alright. Can you come over now? We're at 24th and West Hopkins. See you soon."

As I drove the half hour to the office, I realized that I hadn't seen many White people. There were a few Black men sitting on a nearby bench as I pulled into the parking lot. One nodded at me as they continued their conversation.

I flashed back to my three years at Madison: I'd marched in protests, dodged rocks being tossed at cops, suffered the wrath of pepper spray, and watched fellow students get hit with Billy clubs. I had lived in a volatile enclave off campus where at any time, a perceived injustice could cause the eruption of shouting and often fiery epithets from people whose tempers were already frayed. Soon the police would arrive and work to calm and disperse the crowd until the next outburst.

I had survived all of that, so I certainly could manage spending the summer working in Milwaukee's inner city.

I was ushered into the owner and publisher's office to meet the boss. He stood up from his large wooden desk and shook my hand. He was a tall, lean, nice-looking Black man with an easy smile and a confident stride. I smelled a whiff of Tabu, a cologne my brother wore and that I liked.

Doing my best to look confident, I watched him read my resume. It was a good thing he had a big desk so he couldn't see my hands tightly squeezed together.

He said, "Pretty impressive for a farm girl from Whitewater."

He's not going to hire a White girl. I didn't see any White people when I walked in. I was relieved, though, when the girls typing smiled and acknowledged me.

He asked me about my interest in journalism. I replied that I had been interested in writing for a long time and also enjoyed politics, adding that my desire was to work for a newspaper after graduating.

"Why would a White girl want to work here?" the owner asked.

I thought it best to be honest.

"I had hoped for an internship with a U.S. senator, but it didn't work out at the last minute. I contacted the *Journal* and *Sentinel,* but they'd already filled their intern quotas. I am interested in working for a newspaper and after seeing your listing in the Yellow Pages, I called. So, here I am," I smiled sheepishly.

"Sure you're up for working here? It's not your first choice," he seemed skeptical.

"I would like to give it a try and hope I don't disappoint."

Not getting a good feeling. Maybe I shouldn't have been so honest.

"Come in a week. See you at 8:30," he smiled. I shook his large hand.

"Thank you for giving me this opportunity."

* * *

Telling My Family

Driving back to the farm, I wondered how my parents, sister, and brother would react. My parents were among the first to welcome a Black family to our small town. The husband had accepted a teaching job at the local college. My parents had met them at the United Methodist Church where my parents were long-time members.

Thinking about these events gave me some comfort, but I still wasn't sure my family would be wild about their 19-year-old daughter and sister working in the Inner City. I arrived home after the 90-minute drive just as my father was coming to the house after milking the cows.

The three of us sat down at our round maple dining table. My mother said the blessing and my father dug into the chicken and mashed potatoes.

"So, Sweetie, how'd it go? You're smiling."

"Yes, good news. I got a job. I start next week. With a newspaper called the *Milwaukee Courier*. It's Black-owned and has a very good reputation. I did try the *Sentinel* and *Journal*, but, of course, they'd already hired summer interns."

"What'll you be doing?" Mother asked, looking serious.

"Working in the editorial department, but I'm not sure what else. Hopefully, I'll also get to do some reporting. It'll be a good experience. My boss seemed nice, but I think he could be stern."

"How many other white girls are working there?"

"I'm not sure, Mother. I didn't see any when I went to the office. Guess I'll find out when I start." I suppressed a nervous laugh.

"A man at the office said he had a friend who lives in a really nice area of town on a hill overlooking Lake Michigan. He and his wife have a spare room to rent. I would catch a bus two blocks away." He said it's about a 25-minute ride to the office.

My father finished supper and headed back out to the barn. Not surprisingly, he didn't say anything.

Mother frowned as she cleared the table.

"Well, are you sure you want to do this? I know it's just for the summer, but you know, I'll be worried sick about you. If you're really intent on doing this, I want you to stay in a safe place; I want to speak with the homeowners.

"Just remember: There are a lot of good-looking men out there. I trust that you'll be careful."

Wow! I can't believe she just said that! I didn't even date much at college.

My mother called Diane to tell her about my plans. My sister was concerned for my safety too. She taught art in Waterford, a small nearby town and said that crime in the Milwaukee area had increased in recent months.

My brother had always been very protective of me, so I was prepared for the heavy pushback I got when I called him at the bank where he worked.

"So, Robert, what do you think about your baby sister going to work at a Black-owned newspaper for the summer?" I asked with a teasing voice.

"What! You've got to be joking! Listen, I don't want any man hitting on my beautiful, blue-eyed, blond baby sister. Why put yourself in danger? Want the guys chasing after you? Guess what? I hope you don't get the job."

"Guess what. Too late. I start next week. I'll be careful, I promise. Remember, I've just spent three years at UW. I know you know how crazy that place can be. It's all good. Not to worry." I understood his concerns, but was glad he couldn't see my smirk.

Dodging a Shoot-Out

I thought I had read all there was to know about Black Americans in *The Other America*, *Soul on Ice*, and other books. I knew that Blacks had suffered major set-backs and faced discrimination. It didn't take long for me to realize that reading books couldn't replace actual hands-on experiences and encounters.

The events described here are only a sample of some of those experiences.

After two weeks at the *Courier*, my duties shifted from working in the editorial department to reporting news stories. I was assigned to work with Harvey, a large, jovial man who was the newspaper's photographer. He and Mary, who handled graphic design work, were the only other White people at the paper.

Late one morning, we heard on a police scanner that police were chasing two suspects believed to have just robbed a bank and who were running toward a large cemetery not far from our office. I jumped into Harvey's battered Chevy and we headed toward the cemetery. Sirens were blaring as police cars raced to the scene. Harvey parked along the edge of the cemetery in case we had to make a quick getaway. I followed him, crouching down and hiding behind a tombstone a few feet away.

Quick, staccato bursts of gun shots pierced the air as police shouted for the gunmen to drop their weapons. The noises were getting closer; too close for comfort. I was shaking uncontrollably and, embarrassingly, wet my pants.

"Don't move! Keep your head down!" Harvey whispered more loudly than I thought necessary. After several minutes— which seemed like hours—we heard scuffling, grunts, and other utterances I couldn't quite make out.

Then I heard a loud voice. "Drop your guns! Drop your guns!" Not far away, we could see that several police had tackled two gunmen to the ground.

My legs were very wobbly. Harvey told me to wait in the car while he ran to take pictures of the arrest. I was still shaking when he came back. *If Mother finds out about this, she will be out the door and on her way here to pack me up pronto!*

The whole confrontation had lasted only about 15 minutes, but I was still scared that gunmen might be lurking nearby. Harvey tried his best to calm me down and suggested we grab lunch before heading back to the office. We split a 12-inch turkey and cheese Subway sandwich and talked about what we had witnessed. I hoped that he didn't notice my wet pants.

As I was typing up the story, my boss called me into his office. I didn't like the look on his face.

"Close the door and sit down. Do you know why I called you in here? That was a long lunch. I've got girls out there working and you come wandering in late. What do you think the girls are thinking? 'Yep, white girl can do whatever she wants and gets away with it.' People steal my typewriters and other shit around here and wander in late. I expect that shit to be happening with the other girls, but not from you."

Did he just tell me that being a little late from lunch was the same as stealing a typewriter?

"I'm sorry. Harvey and I were talking about possibilities for the story lead. We lost track of time."

"Tell you what. You're on probation for the next two weeks. It will be lifted if you don't mess up again."

I went back to my desk very upset and angry. The two weeks did pass uneventfully and my probation was lifted. I didn't tell my parents about what had happened.

In early July, they drove to the office. My mother was especially interested in meeting my boss and seeing where I had been working.

"It's a pleasure to meet you, sir. Kay has said so many nice things about you." My mother shook his hand vigorously, though my father offered only a brisk handshake and a nod. I assumed she would be cordial, given that she and my father had been supportive of Blacks as I was growing up. That said, their 19-year-old daughter was working among a mostly Black staff.

He grinned and said how special it was to meet them. "You've done a good job with this one. She's a good reporter. Works hard."

I never knew from day to day what events and stories I would be asked to cover. They were often wide-ranging and impacted me in different ways. Some saddened me, some infuriated me, and some terrified me.

Wild Saturday Night Clash

It was a sweltering Saturday night in mid-July when I was sent to cover a riot. Hundreds of teens and 20-somethings were clashing with police in protest of a recently imposed curfew at "the people's" Water Tower Park. It was a popular gathering spot where kids hung out, especially on balmy summer nights.

I grabbed a discarded pamphlet from the ground. It contained instructions on what to do when confronting the police and urged the rioters to join the fight. I was taken aback by the language.

"Freeing the fountain is the immediate struggle facing our community...We'll use any means necessary to get the pigs off our backs."

Protestors were shouting "free the fountain" and "down with the cops." I stood on the edge of the growing crowd in case I had to make a run for it. Most of the young people looked to be between 16 and 20 years old.

Several boys were standing with their hands in their pockets staring at me. Others had signs saying, "Down with the cops." Two girls were trying to hide their joint. I asked if any of them wanted to comment, as I was covering this event for a newspaper.

"They're trampling on our rights! Kids around here get beaten up every day by the bastards for doing nothing. We're fed up," one of the guys with an Afro yelled, pumping his fist in the air. My brother comes home on leave from the Army and gets blown apart by two white cops. They hate us Black folks." Others nodded.

"Wait, you a reporter for the *Journal?*" Another guy asked, looking angry.

"No, the *Courier*. The Black newspaper," I replied, feeling defensive.

"You some rich White girl bitch pretending to care for us folk. That's what you are. And by the way, you oughta ditch that Army jacket you got on. Not a cool thing in this crowd."

"Who's 'Winn' anyway?" one of the girls bellowed, glaring at me.

I was wearing my brother's Army jacket with our last name on the lapel. Before I could say any more, they ran off toward the center of the mob. The crowd was growing larger and more vocal. Protesters continued to spew anti-cop rhetoric. I was filled with foreboding.

Suddenly, the police fired smoke grenades and pepper gas into the crowd. I quickly covered my face with my bandana. It helped, but my eyes immediately started to water from the pepper gas and my coughing was relentless.

During the anti-war protests in Madison, I had been gassed numerous times; I should have known to carry water. Very few of the protestors were wearing masks or bandanas and many fell to the ground, choking and weeping.

Glass shattered nearby as rocks were thrown at police cars. The police used Billy clubs as they fought and handcuffed kids. I witnessed some of them bleeding after being tossed to the ground. I counted 27 protestors being arrested and taken to the central police station. Others were injured and sent to local hospitals.

By 1:00 AM, the park was deserted, except for police cars posted at several nearby intersections.

In the morning, I headed to the police station to get their perspectives of what had happened during the melee. Tom, a young officer, greeted me. As an ice-breaker, I asked him how long he had been a policeman.

"It'll be two years next week. Started when I was 22," he spoke proudly.

"Congratulations. It takes a lot of courage. Were you at the riot last night?"

"Yeah. Wasn't a good scene. You know, we try to do the right thing. Everyone has a right to protest. But the violence? We don't like to get physical. Last night was rough. I dodged several rocks and got punched before I put a hold on one kid. They can protest; it's their right. But violence isn't necessary. We just try to protect the public."

"What a job you have. Can I quote you for my story?

"I'll have to check with the boss. Can you wait a few minutes?" He came back grinning. "Sure. You know what? My ma will be proud. Wanted me to go to Madison after high school, but I always just wanted to be a cop."

I was so pleased for Tom and his mother, both mentioned in my story. And it was featured on the front page of the next day's paper.

The Woman Needs Help!

As I was working on another story, a large Black woman ambled into our office. Her dress was torn and soiled, and her face was covered with open sores. I had a hard time looking at her, but asked if I could help her.

"I don't know what to do. No money. No doctor will take me." She spoke in a low voice. "Can you help? I'm so sick. Please."

I told her to have a seat and I gave her Styrofoam cup of water. She sat quietly weeping and saying something about "the Lord."

After hearing her story, I called the Milwaukee branch of the National Welfare Rights Organization. I paid for a cab to take her there. Weeks later, I heard that she received medical assistance for advanced venereal disease.

One of the secretaries, a pleasant woman with a big Afro, sounded resigned as she stopped typing and declared, "What you just saw, we see often. We try to help when we can. "

I thought about the sick woman on my way home, feeling very depressed. The staff members seemed to be hardened to the situation because it happened so frequently. How terrible.

Comforting a Mother

One hot July morning, I was told by a colleague to "pick up on line 2." A very distressed male voice was on the phone.

"We've lost our son. Died in the fighting over there, in Vietnam. Was only 19. We don't know anything, except he died last week. The wife, she hasn't stopped crying. We don't know what to do."

I asked him to hold a moment while I checked if the paper published stories about soldiers killed in Vietnam. I told the grieving parents that I would be at their house that afternoon.

I knocked on the screen door and waited. The man, who I assumed was the father, slowly made his way down the narrow wooden stairs. I introduced myself; he did the same. He motioned me to the stairs. Half-way up, panic set in. I wondered for a few seconds if I was putting myself in danger.

All my fears abated quickly as soon as I saw his wife sitting on a faded blue sofa, holding a framed picture of their son in his Army uniform. She wiped her red eyes as she continued to weep. A plastic fan didn't offer much relief from the heat and stuffiness.

"So sorry about your son. What was his name?"

"Melvin. Melvin Franklin Lewis. Franklin for the president," Mr. Lewis declared, with a hint of pride.

"My first-born. Such a good boy. He wanted to join the Army; we couldn't stop him." Mrs. Lewis said as she stared at Melvin's photo. I asked them to tell me what they remembered most about their son.

"Didn't like the books so much. Always wanted to join the Army," the father said, rubbing his hands together.

They both became more talkative as time passed. In the end, I had more than enough information for my story. I asked if they had another picture of their son. If so, it would be printed along with the story. The mother quickly found another one nearby.

"I expect this'll be in next week's edition. If you think of anything you want to add, just call me. Again, I am sorry for your loss." The mother stood up, reached into a bowl of fruit, and gave me an orange. She clasped her hands to her chest.

"Thank you," I said, pushing down the urge to weep too. I had one last story to write.

* * *

As I headed back to the office, it seemed like just yesterday that I had been standing in that hot, smelly phone booth making calls looking for work. My three-month internship seemed to have flown by. And I had learned so much.

After I finished my final story, the staff had a small going-away party for me. A girl my age gave me a note on a small piece of orange paper: "Dear Kay. You are one of the few White folk that has made my mental list of real beautiful people...It makes me feel like there is some hope..."

As I rode the bus home for the last time, I stared at my bus pass. "August 22, 1970." I thought about my summer: cemetery terror, young rioters, my parents' visit, probation, the sick and desperate family losses, and so many more memories. Oh, yes, and "Sugar Britches."

UW GRADUATION (JUNE 1971)

I continued working for the *Daily Cardinal* in my quest to pretty much try everything. That included going to the Badger home football games Saturday afternoons, followed by drinking at some bar, listening to Smokey Robinson, The Who, or Blood, Sweat and Tears, depending on the bar and the hour.

In June 1971, my father, mother, and sister stood proudly at my side for graduation pictures on a warm, sunny day as I received my BA degree in journalism. My father was looking directly at the camera with a tight smile on his face. Little did we know that he would be dead seven months later. My mother was beaming, as was Diane. When reviewing old photos years later, I looked very happy and showed no embarrassment that my black robe was open, showing my cut-off Levis. I was glad to have graduated and was looking forward to my European summer vacation.

Graduation day from the UW with my parents. My roommate Irene (to my left with long brown hair) was my summer travel companion.

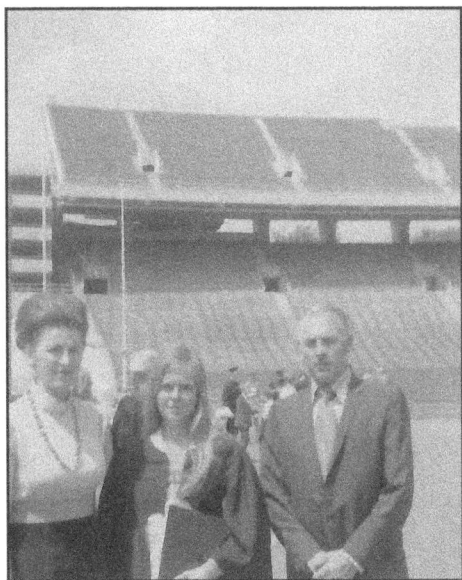

My sister, father, and me at Camp Randall Stadium, Madison, Wisconsin..

EUROPE BOUND

I had made plans with my roommate Irene to travel around Europe for two months shortly after we graduated from UW. However, once we found out how sick my father was, I told my mother that I was going to cancel my trip. She was adamant that I keep my plans.

"You have your life to live. I really think that you should stick to your plans. Just check with American Express offices."

I decided to ask my father's doctor what he thought about my being away for so long.

"I think it would be good for your father psychologically if you go. Just make sure that your mother can reach you." He also said that I should try to enjoy myself saying that this has been "a very difficult time for all of us."

His words sealed the deal so off to Europe Irene and I went with our Eurail passes. We made our way across France, England, Spain, Switzerland, Italy, Germany, and the Netherlands. There were no urgent messages. The few times I called home, Mother said that things were going well. Her letters were filled with news: the tone was unfailingly upbeat and loving. I strongly suspected that wasn't the case, but she always kept up a brave front. My letters to them briefly shared my views about each country, the cities, culture, and food. My letters were the same, upbeat and loving.

The highlights of our travels are in no special order and certainly not comprehensive. However, they are just a snapshot of my observations.

I was nervous about the trip because it was the first time I had travelled on an airplane. I was also excited thinking about what was ahead of us.

Europe, Here We Come!

Irene and I made quite the pair. Two American girls in our early twenties—Irene was a Jersey girl with long black hair, and a trim figure from "New York." I was a blond Wisconsin girl from "California." We figured that it was just simpler for us to introduce ourselves as being from New York and California as most Europeans would more likely have heard of those places.

We began our journey in Brussels. One of the first things that surprised me were the many small, compact cars—VWs and Toyotas—on the roads. It seemed that most people either walked or rode bicycles. The streets and buildings were clean and neat.

Checkpoint Charlie—East Berlin, Germany
The Ugly American—Germany

In Germany, the spoken and unspoken hostilities from the older generations were obvious. However, younger Germans were more friendly. In fact, many were apologetic.

I was riding on a bus on the way to the Berlin train station. I had my purse and bag next to me on an empty seat. Suddenly, an older man and woman stepped inside the bus. The woman grabbed my bags and pushed them onto my lap. She wasn't even going to sit in that seat. She was speaking something in German. Probably "Damned American." I figured that if she hated Americans this much, I would make sure that she would continue to do so. As I got off the bus, I grabbed my suitcase and dragged it across her feet. As much as I wanted to, I didn't look back. I did feel a little ashamed a few days later. The war wasn't over.

Before we entered East Berlin through Checkpoint Charlie, we were required to exchange some dollars for five marks, which we paid to view West Berlin from a tower that overlooked West Germany. All tourists had to spend five marks while visiting. After we finished our visit, I had two marks left and tossed them on the ground before leaving the Checkpoint. I had heard this is what a lot of tourists did.

I had an eerie feeling as we walked down the wide streets; I felt like all eyes were on us. For tourists, there was an area filled with tall buildings and shops. However, one could look beyond this limited space and see clusters of old, empty structures, bombed out and stripped naked from the war.

While we were in the viewing tower, a young boy named Frank, clad in a shirt and pants that looked to be two sizes too large for him, approached us and asked where we were from in a hesitant, shy voice. I thought that he was about ten years old. He spoke a little English.

When we said, "The U.S.," he looked confused, But when we said "America," he quickly replied "Oh, yes!"

He asked many questions. Did we have a car? Could we give him a U.S. dollar? Was West Berlin a big city? We both thought that he was from West Berlin until he showed us a coin from the German Democratic Republic. I thought that Frank's questions were likely ones that other East Berliners wanted to ask.

He kept glancing around as if he knew he shouldn't be talking with us. We were a little leery too.

Guards stood rigidly along the buildings on one side of the main boulevard, while American troops watched from buildings on the other. A guard at Checkpoint Charlie told us the area was the most heavily guarded area in the world, although it was not noticeable because most guards are hidden.

The contrast between the relative bleakness of East Berlin and the apparent wealth of West Berlin was startling. However modern as West Berlin was, I could not forget that very close by were people who could not live their own normal lives. The shoes and hair styles on the women reminded me of the US fashions in the 1950s; low, flat, pointy shoes were worn by most of the women we saw. Bangs and curls seemed to be very popular.

Good and Cheap Flea Markets—Italy

Vendors at the flea markets lining the narrow streets of Florence were selling lots of wonderful leather goods at great bargains. I was travelling on a tight budget so I had to watch how many things I bought, but in Florence, I couldn't help myself. I splurged buying two sweaters for $10, three pairs of gloves for $18, a leather belt for $8, and two nice leather purses for $24.

Besides viewing lots of unique items that could have found their way into my suitcase, Irene and I enjoyed wandering through the open markets and checking out the brightly colored fruits and vegetables, as well as sampling the delicious baked goods.

Bloody Bull Fights—Madrid

I wasn't sure I wanted to watch the bull fights, but it was one of the events I thought I should experience while in Madrid. Excitement filled the air as the trumpets sounded and the matadors marched into the packed, open arena. It wasn't long before the first fight began and blood began to flow from the wounded bull. The blood and gore increased by the minute. I couldn't stand all the blood any longer and began cheering *Olé* for the poor bull. Locals around me frowned and gave me dirty looks. I felt nauseous and depressed.

After the bull had been killed, the crowd cheered and waved white handkerchiefs, indicating that they thought that the matador was very skillful and deserved the bull's ear!

I wondered what good there was in this gory sport so celebrated by the Spaniards, young and old alike. Irene and I left before the fights were over. I had a fleeting thought of a stadium full of cheering Green Packer fans—without the blood, of course—but cheering on rough tackles and quick hits. I decided maybe it's skill that interests many fans.

Carrying My Samsonite

As the days passed, my arms began to ache as I lugged around a tan Samsonite suitcase with no wheels. I weighed it after I returned home. Forty-five pounds! I have my grandfather's trunk that he carried his belongings in when he emigrated from Denmark in 1903. His trunk had metal wheels!

Oh, Those Young and Old Men—Everywhere

Men in all the countries we visited were very forward! All races and colors and shapes. It didn't matter—they stared at us when we wore our cut-offs. They honked their horns.

Some sites from our European adventure.

Ridiculous! Some were really insistent, stopping their cars, jumping out and running along next to us, babbling in Italian. It really got on our nerves. I gave "the elbow" to a few, who quickly scurried away.

European Highlights

There was much rich art, culture, and history to absorb as Irene and I visited famous museums and monuments and viewed master paintings and stunning architecture. I was amazed at the beauty of the Notre Dame Cathedral, the Sistine Chapel ceiling, and St. Peter's Basilica, and all the history of the Roman Forum and the Colosseum.

I recognized the masterworks of Leonardo du Vinci (*Mona Lisa*); Van Gogh (*The Starry Night*) and Munch (*The Scream*). Like so many college dorm walls, I had a *Starry Night* poster on mine. To get the chance to see these beautiful works up close was breathtaking.

We also had memorable times when the countryside, sea, and the mountains provided us with the serenity and quiet beauty of nature. We captured the sunset over Florence; we walked along the shore of the Mediterranean Sea; we viewed the lights of the Eiffel Tower of Paris; we strolled along Lake Lucerne and watched swans gliding on the lake. We gazed at the moon as our train traveled through Switzerland and crossed the Pyrenees Mountains, covered with many green pine trees above the tree line.

As we traveled across Europe, I saw people in the fields raking hay by hand. The farms looked old and small as we passed by. Watching the farmers toiling reminded me of all the times I had helped my father during hay season on our farm.

A New World View

As I traveled through Europe that summer, I was surprised and disappointed by the negative views and comments I heard about America and Americans from fellow travelers. My eyes were opened and my pride at being an American was punctured.

However, as I began my professional career and interacted with people of different nationalities and customs, I realized how much I had actually learned and benefited from my foreign travel. Some of my realizations were:

- Don't take our freedoms for granted.
- Be open to dissent. Learn to listen to and appreciate different views/cultures.

- Accept that not everyone respects or likes Americans.
- Strive to live and work to be a good, not an ugly, American. Reputations are important around the world.
- Learn from history.
- War had consequences.
- Strive to get a better understanding and an increased awareness of other countries and their governments.

Future Travels

Years later, my mother and I visited her ancestral home in Denmark. I believe I got my love of exploring other cultures from her.

Mother in Denmark (1979)

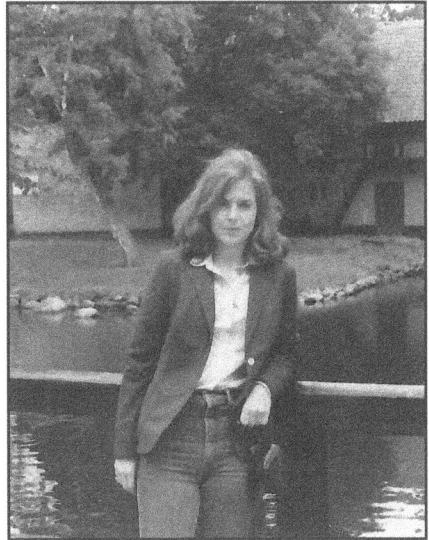

Me in Denmark (1979)

MY FATHER'S TEARS

Within a week of my returning home from Europe, a phone call came with the news that my father's mother, Huldah, had died after suffering from cancer; her five-foot frame had shrunk to next to nothing. It was the first and only time I ever saw my father shed a tear, but he didn't say anything and headed out the door to the barn. He had visited his parents frequently, especially after they moved to Whitewater so they could be closer.

"TONIGHT ALONE"

My Father's Illness

The doctor looked me straight in the eye.

"Your father has a rare form of leukemia called multiple myeloma. It's treatable, but not curable. He's in the advanced stages. I just got the test results this morning. They weren't the results any of us wanted," Dr. Waters spoke in a soft voice. He reached across and patted my hand.

We were sitting in chairs outside my father's room at the Methodist Hospital in Madison.

"Wish I had better news. I'm sorry for you all. We'll do whatever we can to help your father fight this."

I was in disbelief. Tears started flowing. I felt faint.

I thought losing a parent would happen when I was forty and married with two children.

"So, what does that mean? How long does he have?" My voice trembled.

"Between six months and two-and-a-half years," the doctor said in a quiet tone, almost a whisper.

I knew my dad wasn't well, because the frequent blood transfusions didn't seem to help him, but such a dire prognosis shocked me. I had promised my mother that if I heard the results of the tests before she did, I would tell her. I had to keep my word.

Dr. Waters stood up, tall and lanky, and gave me a hug. He had known our family for many years. He went on. "I have to speak at a conference tomorrow, but will be back by 5:00. I'll talk with your mother in the lobby of Methodist Hospital about what this all means and what the next steps might be. I'll also be available anytime your sister, brother, and you want to talk. See you and your mother tomorrow."

Dr. Waters had trained at the Mayo Clinic before joining the clinic connected to the hospital. He was the doctor who had finally diagnosed my father's disease, which up until then had other physicians guessing.

Ominous Signs

At 55, my father had never been sick, other than suffering from hay fever. The local doctors had prodded, poked, and injected him with steroids, repeatedly trying to treat what they had determined was arthritis. The diagnosis was later modified to include anemia, thought to be the culprit in my father's lack of energy. Prednisone was given for pain.

An entire year went by before my mother was able to convince my father to see a specialist.

For months, sudden nosebleeds had left his handkerchiefs and shirts caked and stained. His coughing and spitting up gunk became more frequent. Purple splotches slowly spread over his thin arms. His energy level left him increasingly unable to get all the cows milked without help from neighbors.

As the cancer progressed, his hospital stays became more frequent. Our conversations focused on farm-related issues that my father wanted addressed. Even with the symptoms and the poor prognosis, my mother's optimism was firm. She kept telling me that he would get better.

"Everything's going to be alright," she said, month after month.

* * *

When my father came to Madison for his monthly blood transfusions, I'd walk the ten minutes to the hospital from my office at the State Capitol. That day, as I walked back to the sorority house where I lived, everything seemed distorted. The WALK/DON'T WALK signs looked like they were smeared with Vaseline. My tears kept flowing.

I called my mother at work as soon as I got back to my desk. I told her that Dad was tolerating the blood transfusions.

"Hello, Mother. I ran into Dr. Waters. We didn't talk long, He's speaking at a conference tonight, but will talk with us tomorrow at the hospital."

* * *

"Mother, I have to work late, but I'll meet you in the lobby. Remember, I told you that I would go home with you to attend a baby shower for Becky."

As our car sliced through the darkness along Interstate 90 between Madison and Whitewater, my mother stared straight ahead. I asked her how the hired man was handling all the chores, and how her students were doing. Her answers were terse and detached.

"You saw Dr. Waters. What'd he say? Any test results yet?" she asked firmly.

"Well, yes. He said ..." I hesitated and cleared my throat.

"Tell me the truth. Just be honest." She sounded resolved.

"OK. Well, he said that Dad is in the advanced stages of whatever is making him sick. He called it multiple myeloma, a rare form of leukemia. It's treatable, but not curable. He could live between six months and two-and-a-half years."

I glanced at her quickly out the corner of my eye. Dry-eyed and looking straight ahead, she only said, "Thank you."

"Dr. Waters said he wished he had better news for us, but would do whatever he can to help Dad."

Ever Optimistic

My mother was cheerful even under the most uncheerful conditions. I remember my Aunt Evie telling me that "she was good at not facing anything she didn't want to hear. She would ignore things if she didn't believe them."

My mother was always proud that our father knew how to ask for church donations. "I could never ask anyone for money," she said.

Her usual refrain was "He was a good man. He tried. Worked hard and looked after his parents. I do miss him. So young, only 57. He shouldn't have suffered like he did."

She always said that she was very blessed to have three healthy children and husband.

"That's all I can ask for," she often told the three of us.

Diane, Robert, and me (1 year old)

THE LETTER TO EVIE

While going through old documents for this book, I found a copy of a letter my mother had written to Evie a week after my father passed away.

> *Dear Evie, there are three milestones now where my world has really changed. 1. Leaving home at nine to go to Rochester* [boarding school]*, 2. Driving away from home with Jay* [to elope]*, and 3. Tonight alone. Time has been filled since you left, but every so often a peculiar wave of fear passes over me."*

My sadness was immediate as I stared at her words. Such profound grief and loneliness expressed in so few words.

"Tonight alone."

I read the letter again. Why hadn't I taken more of an interest in my mother's life? How many ancient wounds had she buried deep inside?

Why she had kept a copy of the letter? Maybe she wanted to save it to read again for mysterious reasons. Or maybe she wanted me to find it, read it, and ask myself if hurts were ever in the past tense.

GOODBYE, FATHER

My father died two years after his original diagnosis of multiple myeloma. On a frigid Wisconsin January day, my mother, sister, brother, and I attended his funeral. We shuffled along the ice-covered sidewalk and entered the United Methodist church in Whitewater and took our places at the front of the chapel. White lilies and red carnations covered the coffin.

This was the church where funerals were held for both of my parents and where Diane was married. It was also the church where I was confirmed and attended Sunday School taught by my mother. My father often raised money for the church and was a reliable usher.

I was pleasantly surprised by the number of men and women who filled the pews for the service. There had also been a steady stream at his visitation the night before. I didn't realize that my father had been so well liked by local farmers, college professors, local Democrats, and members of the church. The sounds of organ music filled the chapel. Occasionally, they were punctuated by coughs and sniffles. During the service, I glanced at my mother seated next to me.

Was Mother crying? No tears? She's being stoic.

Diane wiped tears from her eyes. Robert stared ahead most of the time.

I thought about the night before at the visitation as I stood by my mother as she grasped the hands of grown men. She comforted them and told them how much my father appreciated them as they fought back tears.

No tears. I didn't cry either. I guess I wanted to be strong for my mother. I thought about telling her about the note I had slipped into my father's coffin the night before.

Dear Daddy,
Mother, Diane, Robert, and I, Sissie and Princess, will always love you.

I had rarely talked to my mother about my father as his illness consumed him. I don't think that my sister and brother did either. I thought that if I asked her questions about how she was coping or expressed my sadness, it would upset her even more.

Why should I encourage her to talk about such sad times?

Looking back, it seems incomprehensible and irresponsible that I didn't encourage her to talk and share her feelings about my father's illness and death, or even to remember the good times.

LUCKY AND VICKI—
THE COMPASSION OF ANIMALS

The day my father passed away of cancer was the same day that our Morgan horse, Lucky, died near the front door of our barn. For more than fifteen years, Lucky had almost always been at my father's side, following him around without needing reins. My father had a hot temper, but he loved Lucky.

Vicki, a horse we took in when her owners moved, got pregnant by a neighbor's horse that broke through a fence. Vicki was already old and lost the newborn; my father disposed of the stillborn foal promptly. For days, Vicki and Lucky stood over the cold ground where she had given birth. The two horses just stood there in their corral, heads bowed, their eyes wet and matted. They didn't move to the shelter where they usually ate and slept. The shelter protected them from the freezing Wisconsin weather.

My father carried bales of hay and buckets of water to them, but they wouldn't eat or drink. It saddened me to see them out in the cold mourning.

He put some old blankets on them. "Maybe it'll help. I did try to coax Lucky to see if he would move, but he didn't. He just shuffled his hooves in place, so I left him alone. When I feed them in the morning, I will try again."

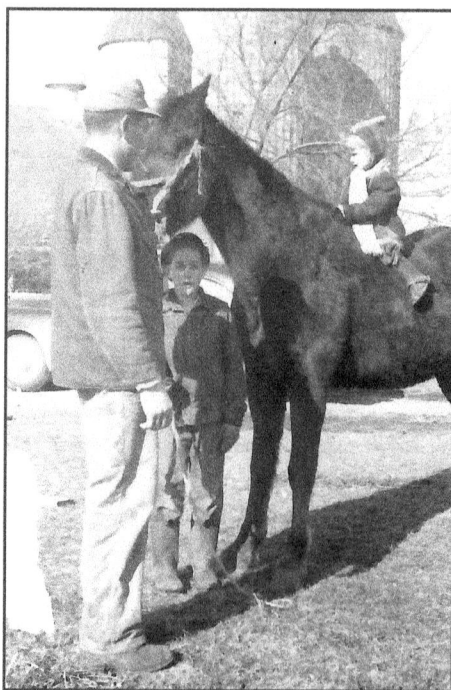

Me as a toddler on Lucky. Robert is
looking on. Dad is holding the halter.

TIME FOR THE BIG-GIRL BOOTS

THE WISCONSIN DEMOCRATIC ASSEMBLY CAUCUS

After I returned from Europe, I sent out more than 40 resumes, hoping that my journalism degree and resume would open the door for journalism-related opportunities, such as writing or reporting for a newspaper. The national inflation rate was 8.8%; needless to say, companies weren't hiring. I didn't have any luck, though I did receive one response from the *Christian Science Monitor* and a small, not-for-profit organization. Neither had any openings.

Discouraged but not giving up, I took a job as a page in the Wisconsin Democratic Assembly Caucus. I quickly realized that I wasn't going to make being a page my career and began to work for an assemblyman from the Milwaukee area writing press releases and speeches.

OFF TO D.C.

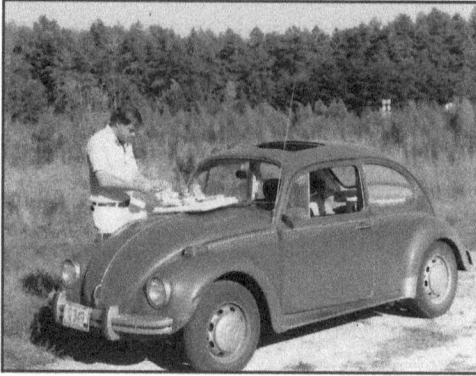

Heading to the Big City.

I was filled with excitement and anxiety as I drove along Interstate 90 in my red 1970 VW Beetle headed to D.C. to start a new job working in the U.S. House of Representatives.

I had flown to Washington three weeks earlier for an interview. I didn't know anyone so I didn't have my hopes up, but because of my mother's encouragement, I interviewed and shortly thereafter, I was offered the job.

dSG DEMOCRATIC STUDY GROUP • U.S. HOUSE OF REPRESENTATIVES
225-5858 • 1422 HOUSE OFFICE BUILDING • WASHINGTON, D.C. 20515

HON. BOB ECKHARDT (Tex.)—Chairman   RICHARD P. CONLON—Staff Director

Dear Grandpa:

Mother probably told you that I spent last week-end in Milwaukee helping the Jimmy Carter campaign. While I do find faults with him, I think that he would make a good President. I frankly resent the fact that HHH is sitting the whole primary process out, and then be granted the nomination on a silver platter. That makes our whole primary system into a farce. At any rate, I was xxxxxx very happy at the Carter victory. He has a very dedicated, small, but very organized staff, and I certainly enjoyed the opportunity to help out. I had hoped that they would have asked me to Pennsylvania this week-end, as I would have gone in a flash. That state is key.....

Partial letter to my grandfather.

A Texas-sized TV filled most of the back seat. All my other scant belongings were stuffed any place there was space. My mother was wedged in the front seat. Every now and then as a car passed us, the driver honked. They saw my bumper sticker that read "Honk if you think he's guilty." ("He" meant President Nixon.) We know how that turned out.

The year was 1973. I had just left my job in Madison to join a staff of eight in in the House of Representatives called the Democratic Study Group (DSG). It functioned as a policy resource for liberal and moderate Democratic members of Congress and their staff. We helped draft legislation and produced fact sheets and reports pending in committees or on the House floor.

Standing in front of the nation's Capitol in Washington, D.C. Short dresses and long hair were all the rage when I worked on Capitol Hill.

You're Hired

My new boss told me as we sat in his office that I would be covering "energy issues." I fessed up that I didn't know anything about energy. This concerned me, but I said that I was ready to learn. My lack of knowledge obviously didn't bother him. Neither was the fact that I was a sweaty mess sitting in front of him wearing a heavy fake-fur winter coat. It was 80 degrees outside; the temperature in Wisconsin had been 40 degrees when I boarded my flight in Milwaukee earlier that November day. I learned quickly about what people called an "Indian summer."

The *New York Times* article highlighted the development of a national energy policy, on which I worked with senior staff.

He directed me to my new work station. It was a small cubicle with a chair, a desk, and two olive-green metal filing cabinets. As he was leaving, he looked directly at me and said to get ready to work. "Good luck. Get to work. Lots going on."

Time to Take on the Challenge

Indeed, these were unexpected and challenging times. I was chewed out more than once by congressmen or their staff. In one instance, I made a stupid mistake misrepresenting a member's position on a draft energy bill that was important to one of his big donors. They were unintentional mistakes, but being on the receiving end of a rant by a congressman, with my boss standing next to him glaring at me, made my teeth rattle.

Would firing me be far off?

It wasn't long before I felt unwelcomed by several of my colleagues. I'm sure that they thought I was just a dumb farm girl from Wisconsin. This didn't help my confidence in tackling the energy policy portfolio. I decided to just be polite and mind my own business. I kept my head down. My cubicle became my safe place—or so I thought.

One afternoon, when I returned from attending a congressional hearing, I found chewed gum jammed into the locks on the two filing cabinets. All I heard were muffled snorts. I did figure out how to remove the gum and was able to use the filing cabinets.

Even though some of my new colleagues acted in unkind and petty ways, I liked my job. I made valuable contacts and learned a lot. My eyes were opened and my backbone stiffened.

Farm Girl Heads to the White House

After working for two years in the U.S. House of Representatives at the Democratic Study Group, a former colleague asked me if I wanted to work in the White House focusing on energy-related issues. Of course, I couldn't pass up the chance. This 25-year-old Wisconsin farm girl was headed to the White House to work with a small team of very bright experts striving to tackle the energy crisis.

The crisis had been caused by the so-called Arab oil embargo in 1973, when Arab oil exporters imposed a temporary cessation of oil shipments from the Middle East to the US and many of its allies. This was in retaliation for American support of Israel during the Yom Kippur War.

One Proud and Happy Mother

I was excited to tell my mother the news. I called her during her lunch break.

"Mother, you won't believe this! Are you sitting down?"

"Everything alright, Sweetie?"

"Yes, for sure! I'm going to work at the White House! I just found out. I start in three weeks. I'm scared, but so, so excited. I'll be a junior staffer working directly with ten or so energy experts.

"Wonderful news! I always knew you would go places. Can't wait to tell my friends my daughter is working in the White House. Wow! Your father would have been so proud too."

"But, you know what, Mother. I will be the same person. This isn't going to my head. Of course, it will be a lot of long hours. I hope I can do the job."

"You're going to do fine. Just make sure your seams are straight." (Back then, stockings with seams running up the back were popular.) She laughed.

The Energy Crisis Hits America

President Jimmy Carter went on television and spoke to "his fellow Americans," declaring that the energy crisis in the U.S. demanded immediate and focused attention. The administration's goal was to craft the nation's first national energy policy, with the aim of increasing U.S. supplies, reducing demand, and creating a Cabinet-level Secretary of Energy. President Carter said that he wanted this accomplished within three months.

American drivers were experiencing long gas lines as supplies dropped. Gas prices surged. Tempers flared at gas stations. Americans loved their gas-guzzling cars; the notion that gasoline was scarce, or even unavailable, was a shock. We were used to just pulling up to a gas station and filling up.

The second shock to the world oil market occurred after Iran ousted the Shah, the last monarch, in 1979, The country's oil production dropped and the Organization of Petroleum-Exporting Countries (OPEC) raised prices, triggering another shortage.

Pressure to Produce

Our work was cut out for us and the pressure to produce results was intense. The experts often worked 14 to 16 hours a day, seven days a week. I was a junior staffer, so I got Sundays off. That wasn't much time to hang out with friends; all I wanted to do on Sunday was sleep. I worked primarily as a liaison between the White House and members of Congress and their staff who were interested in energy policy. It was challenging and stressful; I often felt overwhelmed by the competing views. Nevertheless, there was a lot of collaboration with outside groups and special interests as we crafted legislation and developed policies. Oil and gas industry representatives, labor unions, environmentalists, and consumer groups were a few of those seeking to have their views heard.

THE FRENCH DIPLOMAT

"Meet me at the Mayflower Hotel bar at 6:00 PM tonight."

I stared at my phone, surprised to get this voice-mail message from one of my bosses at the White House.

What an odd request. Meet at a bar? Why not in his office?

I had two hours to fret.

Is this something to do with my job, I wondered.

It was an intense time, but I hadn't gotten any negative feedback about my work from him or anyone else, for that matter. He frequently sat in for at least part of our meetings. On occasion, I briefed him in his office about an issue or sought his advice. He had an aura of strength and toughness about him that kept staff on their toes.

The Wait Begins

I was first to arrive at the bar and slid into a booth. When I was meeting someone, I always liked to get seated first and attempt to get settled before the other party arrived. I quickly looked in my mirror to see if I had on enough lipstick and my hair was half-way decent.

I had a pen and pad of paper in case I needed to take notes. It was always handy for me to clench a pen under the table. For some odd reason, I convinced myself it lessened my anxiety in meetings.

This is all so weird.

As I sat there, I remembered being taken aback during our interview for the position at the White House. He looked directly at me. "Can you type?"

Can I type? Really?

It was 1978. No one had asked me that since my typing teacher in high school years before.

Was this a joke? Looking for a reaction?

"Yes, I can type, but it's been a while." I was careful as he didn't express any emotion.

I thought back about that exchange. In a few minutes, that same man was going to be sitting across from me.

Tom, my boss, arrived a few minutes later. He was well built, with a trim waistline and muscular hands that looked like they could crack rocks. No doubt, he could swiftly lay waste to anyone if the need arose.

He apologized for his tardiness and was very gracious, as always. He ordered a wine spritzer for me; he had a whiskey. Or maybe it was bourbon.

"How's work going?"

"I work. I sleep. That's about it. No fun these days, but I can't complain. It's stressful, but I love it."

"So, no boyfriend?"

"No, just work, like I said. Any problem with my work?" I hope he didn't detect any attitude.

Let's get on with whatever this is about.

"Not at all. You work hard and are reliable. We're lucky to have you helping us. Crazy times." He took a swig of whatever he was drinking.

"I'm sure you're wondering why I asked you to meet me. There's someone I would like you to meet. It's a sensitive situation, so please keep our conversation between us."

Why a secret?

The need for secrecy perplexed me. I kept a poker face, but gave my pen a tight squeeze under the table.

"He was a high-ranking Soviet diplomat who recently defected from Russia to seek asylum here. He just wanted out. I'm just trying to help him get settled."

I thought he said that the man was a "diplomat," but the bar was noisy so I wasn't sure. I figured things would become clearer before too long.

I had never heard of this man before, but why would I?

Something held me back from asking how he knew the Russian, but I was curious. I heard my mother sitting on my shoulder saying, "Keep your mouth shut. People love to talk about themselves."

I suddenly remembered that a colleague told me shortly after I started working at the White House that Tom's background was "intelligence." He had won numerous awards for bravery fighting in World War ll.

Was there some connection between the two?

My boss said, "He's a decent man. As you can imagine, he would like to meet a lady as a companion. I thought you might enjoy meeting him."

"His stories must be awesome." I smiled, squeezing my pen.

This could be a cool adventure! What an amazing man to write about!

I looked at Tom. "Maybe I could wear a wire under my blouse, record his stories, and write about his life. What do you think?" I smiled.

"It wouldn't be a good idea. Remember that he's looking for a lady to spend time with. A companion."

I sat there, thinking to myself, *Why would this famous man want to have dinner with me?* I was a blue-eyed, blond farm girl, but certainly not anywhere near a Washington sophisticate. There were a lot of those from which to choose.

"If I had dinner with him, would the Russians be watching us or just me? Would I be in danger?" I asked hesitantly.

Again, I didn't recall the precise answer, but Tom said something like the Russians didn't miss much.

I definitely felt like I would have to be careful when I met this Russian. Maybe even when I wasn't with him. I wasn't getting a good feeling about this.

"I don't expect an answer now. I know it's a lot to absorb," Tom said.

"Sounds interesting, but scary too. I wish I could record our conversations though. I need time to think about this. To be honest, the Russians scare me. You know, the Cold War and all."

"Just so it's clear, you would be spending time with him in his apartment. He'll want you to stay over sometimes. A companion."

"You mean I would have to sleep with this man? Seriously?" My heart skipped a beat.

Why would I agree to sleep with a Russian? I couldn't even tape our conversations!

"I'm sorry, Tom, but why would you think this is something I would agree to do? Never mind. No need to answer." I kept my mouth shut; I had to go to work the next day.

* * *

It wasn't long after my meeting with Tom at the Mayflower Bar that Judy Chavez, a 22-year-old escort service hostess, began a summer-long romance with Mr. Shevchenko. Ms. Chavez said publicly that the romance began when a supposed FBI agent ordered a call girl for the Russian. According to Ms. Chavez, the agent requested a woman to entertain a "French diplomat." Shortly after meeting, the two traveled, dined, and shopped together with federal funds, according to Ms. Chavez. (The "diplomat") was given a new identity by the U.S. government.)

After their summer affair, Ms. Chavez abruptly ended it and charged publicly that she was being paid by the CIA to provide sex for the diplomat. The following year, she published a book called *Defector's Mistress – The Judy Chavez Story*."

The ensuing publicity considerably troubled Mr. Shevchenko, according to press accounts. He continued living in D.C., but disappeared from public view. The press reported that after he defected, his wife returned to Russia and committed suicide. Press reports at the time also relayed that Ms. Chavez lived in Georgetown in Washington D.C. along with a fish tank full of piranhas.

CLUELESS

The thought of becoming a diplomat's mistress triggered some memories. Years earlier, I was a jealous young woman and just as clueless.

Maybe it was young love. I still don't know why I took a big liking to Bill back in high school and college. He was pudgy—not athletic—but a nice guy. I was pudgy then too, the type of girl the boys poked fun at in their locker room. I could just hear them. "Well, but she's got a nice personality."

Bill had been the first chair flutist in our Whitewater High School band. The family's brick house with white shutters also had a large oval swimming pool in the backyard. His father drove a shiny black Cadillac and sold equestrian items in his shop.

Bill hung out with my girlfriends who lived nearby him in town; I was very envious of the time they spent together, especially while I was stuck doing farm chores.

Some school nights after the cows were milked, I would borrow my parent's car, telling them I was going to the public library in town. I drove past Bill's house to see if he was home. Our town was small enough that I could make my way quickly through the streets in my quest if he wasn't home. Of course, I never wanted to get caught snooping, but I just had to know what he was doing.

I did think it was odd that he didn't have many guy friends. Maybe it was because he wasn't a jock. Was he too pudgy?

* * *

After we graduated from high school, Bill went on to study music at the University of Wisconsin–Milwaukee; I headed to the UW-Madison and planned to study journalism. The two campuses were an hour and a half from each other. We saw each other every few weeks in either city or met at his house or our farm.

One weekend in November in my sophomore year, he invited me to a dance at the UW–Milwaukee. I was excited about going. I suggested that we stay in a hotel, as he didn't have an extra room at his apartment and, besides, this was going to be a special weekend. We might kiss and play around!

He greeted me at the hotel with flowers and waited in the lobby while I put on my new outfit. It had cost more than I ever paid for an outfit: a light blue pullover top with a zipper down the front and madras bell-bottoms. I felt special; I didn't think that I looked pudgy.

We were both in good moods when we arrived at the dance. He introduced me to a couple of friendly women, which helped calm my nerves.

We arrived back at the hotel around 11:30 PM. We sat and chatted about the dance and his friends.

I moved closer to him on the sofa and reached for his hand.

"Why's your hand so sweaty?" he chuckled.

After half an hour, I said that I was going to get ready for bed. I went to our room and changed into my blue pajamas and a light robe; I climbed on the bed. Bill soon joined me; he was also in his pajamas.

"Why do you have so many layers on?" he asked. He tugged at my robe as he pulled out a Bible from a nightstand on his side of the bed.

This is very weird. I don't have a good feeling about this.

We both were quiet for several minutes. I stared at the ceiling, but glanced at him out of the corner of my eye.

Should I do this? I'm nervous.

I went for it and slowly rolled over toward him.

"I knew you would do that! What would our mothers think?" he smirked.

* * *

One day, when we were having lunch together, I asked my brother Robert if he thought Bill liked boys. Now I knew— Robert had been right when he said that I would know when Bill and I got in bed and nothing happened.

* * *

I rolled back to my side of the bed. "Good night."

The next morning, nothing was said about the night before. We decided to have breakfast at a favorite place near his apartment before I headed back to our farm.

Bill had recently moved to a new apartment that I hadn't seen before. He invited me in for quick look before I headed out. As I was leaving, I had a feeling that he was stalling, that he had something he wanted to tell me. I asked for a glass of water, thinking the extra minutes might give him time to get up the nerve to tell me whatever it was.

"I have something to tell you," he struggled. "I like boys. Maybe you figured it out. I'm sorry."

He fought back tears. *Was it a mixture of sadness and relief?*

I didn't know what to say. I remembered again what my brother had said.

Bill told me that he would like to take me to a gay bar the next time I visited. I said I would think about it.

That idea scared me. I tried to absorb it all.

I wanted to be supportive, but I had very mixed feelings. I still couldn't find the words to respond, except my first question was, "Do you slow dance?"

I thanked him for telling me and gave him a quick hug.

"I hope you're happy." I tried to smile.

* * *

On my hour-and-a-half drive home, my mind was bombarded with confusion, sadness, doubts. I felt a loss. So much for me to absorb.

How could I have missed all the signs? How many red flags? Talk about clueless!

I arrived at our house, walked in, and burst out crying. My mother gave me a hug. My father asked if something happened to the car and if I was okay; my mother replied that the car was fine.

"She's okay, but she doesn't want to talk about it now. It's something to do with Bill. As soon as she finishes with a shower, I'm driving her back to Madison. I am hoping that she'll talk about whatever it is that has her so upset."

As Mother drove along Highway 12, I still couldn't make sense of how stupid I had been. I wondered what would happen to Bill.

"I understand how upset you are, Sweetie. Bill's a very nice young man, but it's best that he has told you. You know, his being gay doesn't need to be an issue that splits up your friendship. You like Bill; he's a kind guy. Still, I know it's a shock to you."

I turned to her and asked, "Did you tell Dad?"

"Yes. He didn't say much."

"What'd Robert say?"

He said, "It was about time you figured it out."

* * *

Long after college, I learned that Bill was living somewhere in Pennsylvania caring for his mother and singing in a men's chorus. I was living in Washington D.C. working in the federal government. We hadn't spoken for quite a long time.

Bill called out of the blue one evening. I wasn't in the mood for a long chat as I was struggling with a very difficult romantic break-up.

Two days later, he and his boyfriend were waiting for me on the front steps of my townhouse on Capitol Hill.

"You sounded terrible on the phone. I'm here to check up on you. So, what's the deal with this guy who's hurt you? Do I need to find him and have strong words?"

"No, she's gone and it's for the best."

STILL NO WORDS

It was the quickness of the steps that caught my ear. Someone was next to me all of a sudden. I stepped to the right side of the sidewalk to let him go by. He looked O.K. White shirt. Tie. Black dress shoes.

He slowed his pace. *Maybe he's going to ask me for directions,* I thought. He didn't say anything. His fist slammed into the left side of my face. I froze.

What does he want? Ask me for something. Anything! Did he want my jewelry? Money? Does he just want to hurt me? Why?

Still no words.

Why wouldn't he speak?

Another blow.

The groceries I had just purchased from a nearby corner store spilled onto the sidewalk. I fell onto the grass next to a parked car and cowered in the fetal position. Instinctually, I covered my face and breasts. He kicked me. My head was throbbing. The grass was damp from a recent rain and it was beginning to get dark on this early September evening.

Is he going to kill me? Will he shoot or stab me? Probably stab me; it would be quieter than a gun shot. Will he try to rape me?

This total stranger clearly wanted to harm me; I was trapped and hurting. I was overwhelmed with fear.

Still no words.

I had to scream or else he might kill me. *You can do this,* I told myself. Maybe a Senate staffer from the nearby Senate office building will hear me.

"Help me! Help me!'" I screamed and I wept.

Still no words.

"Are you alright? I just saw a man run away. Did he attack you?" a voice asked. I was shaking. He draped his jacket over me.

"He went that way." I pointed in the direction and realized that my arm was swollen and painful. My head throbbed. Two more Senate staffers comforted me. I was embarrassed; I had wet my pants. Maybe they'll think it's from the damp grass.

Sirens. Police. Flashing lights. Two Capitol Hill police squatted next to me. I told them what had happened as they looked at my face and arms. They told me that an ambulance was on its way.

That's Him

"We detained a man a few blocks away. Think you could identify him?" I was scared but agreed to look. I slumped in the back seat of the cruiser in increasing pain.

"All I know is he had on hard shoes." As soon as I spoke, I wondered what would have happened if he had been wearing sneakers, rather than heavy dress shoes?

Maybe it was just because he was so big. What if he hadn't really been wearing a white shirt? Tie? What if he wasn't really that big?

The police car pulled up near where he was handcuffed against the trunk of another cruiser. He stared right at me. I quickly looked at him, then away. I glanced at his shoes and like a window shade being slowly pulled up, my eyes traveled upward. Hard black dress shoes. Dark pants. White shirt. Tie. His eyes were fixed on me.

Still no words.

"That's him! Take him away," I said in a meek voice.

Then I was taken to the hospital where I saw a neurologist, who immediately sent me for a CAT scan and x-rays of my skull and upper torso. I also met with an eye specialist to check the contusion over my right eye. Fortunately, all the tests were negative, but it took months for the facial cuts to heal and the purple bruises to disappear.

I was kept at the hospital overnight as a precaution. I ached all over, even though I had been given pain medicine. It made me drowsy, but I still decided to call my mother. I told her briefly what had happened and that I had some bruising and ached, but fortunately all the tests came back okay. I didn't go into detail because she was already upset.

"You've had rotten luck. I worry about you so much in that city. I'll try to get a flight out tomorrow, Sweetie."

"Oh, Mother, there's no need to come. The doctors are doing a good job of looking after me. I'll call you tomorrow and give you an update. Besides, Doug is here and I'm going to his house."

I hung up thinking that I shouldn't have called her, but nothing really happened in my life that she didn't know about. She's always been my rock.

Months passed before the court summons arrived. My attacker was seated in the front of the courtroom. His head was bowed. No eye contact was just fine with me. He took the stand first.

"Your Honor, I allowed myself to be served one too many drinks at an office party ... I did stalk her. ... I am sorry."

One of the Senate staffers who had comforted me after the attack had offered to serve as a witness. He approached the bench and began to answer questions from the judge.

"Your Honor, the victim cried out, 'Help! Help me!' She sounded like a trapped, defenseless animal. She was in terrible distress. Her face was already bruising. She looked stunned."

The judge then called on me. I approached the bench and read my victim impact statement, which stated in part:

> *"Suddenly, I realized that this person clearly wanted to hurt me. I was overwhelmed with fear. He asked for no money, no sex. He said nothing. Clearly, I realized with a great deal of fear that this person, this total stranger, intended to harm me."*

He had no prior record and held a steady job fixing computers for congressional staff. He was also honorably discharged from the military: his lack of a prior record allowed him to receive a light sentence—only 60 days in jail on weekends.

The prosecutor told me that his decision was based, in part, on the strength of my victim impact statement. If I had been less clear, he might have gone completely free. A policeman who was at the scene and saw my face told me later that if the beatings to my face and torso had continued unabated, that I could have been seriously injured or worse, killed.

Those terrifying few minutes on a mild September night in Washington D.C. have stayed with me over many years. I lived two blocks from where the assault took place approximately 15 blocks from where he lived. I worried that he would find out where I lived and take revenge. There are court records after all. I was healed physically, but my fears lingered.

I often worried that someday he would show up at my front door. That never happened, but even years later, I still cowered when I walked down a street and heard footsteps fast approaching from behind me. I immediately flashed back to those dress shoes and that stranger beside me.

My sudden cowering scared more than one unsuspecting person walking past me on a busy city street. Some men took my elbow trying to be helpful. Others looked at me suspiciously and quickly moved away. I knew what they must have been thinking: *That person's not well.*

If they only knew.

MOVING INTO THE PRIVATE SECTOR / GOING IT ALONE

A New Challenge

After ten years of working in state and federal governments and the private sector, I decided it was time for a change. I had worked in the Wisconsin State Assembly, the U.S. House of Representatives, the White House, the U.S. Department of Energy (DOE), and in the Washington D.C. office of a Fortune 500 energy company headquartered in Houston. I planned to go out "my own" and establish my one-woman government relations (GR) firm—Kathleen Winn & Associates (KW&A)—with offices located in D.C. and Toronto.

I thought that my extensive government experience would equip me with the tools to provide valuable services for clients. I also had letters of recommendations from the Speaker of the House Tom Foley, Secretary of Defense Les Aspin, and a senior DOE official. My boss in the private sector for eight years also wrote a very positive letter.

My goal was to offer strategic advice to Canadian companies interested in engaging with U.S. federal government officials. I would also keep them apprised of legislative and regulatory actions on issues of importance to their companies, as desired. If, for example, a Canadian company was interested in a particular issue in the US related to cross-border or energy activities, KW&A would act on the company's behalf and develop a strategic plan depending on their needs. The plan would include identifying the appropriate congressional staff for handling the issue, as well as DOE and Department of Transportation (DOT) staff, and set up meetings to advocate on the company's behalf. Energy-related meetings would be held at the DOE, and the cross-border issue, at the DOT.

I also worked with U.S. companies operating in Canada seeking to understand how the Canadian government functioned and to monitor selected initiatives.

My colleagues and friends were surprised when I told them about my new challenge. They wished me well, but I don't believe that they expected me to pull it off. I worked hard (I learned that on our farm.), but I think they felt, "Be kind, but don't encourage her." There was a lot of competition for government work in D.C., especially when it was just a middle-aged me. Two well-regarded GR veterans were my associates; they were helpful those times when I needed extra assistance.

A big part of my motivation to establish KW&A was the desire to have more freedom in my professional and personal life. I always welcomed the opportunities to work

Kathleen Winn & Associates

with interesting and dedicated colleagues and to learn a broad range of issues over the years, but I was tired of working for others. I suffered from burn-out and wanted control of my own schedule. I also welcomed the opportunity to be able to head to Whitewater from D.C. or Toronto and to have more time to spend with friends and family. This flexibility was especially important because my mother was suffering from early-onset dementia and resided in an assisted living facility in my hometown. She wasn't going to get any better.

To lobby for U.S. companies, I had to sign up with the U.S. federal government as a "registered lobbyist." For Canadian companies seeking U.S. assistance, I had to register as a "foreign agent." Lobbyists and GR consultants are often called the same. Lobbying is a form of advocacy that lawfully attempts to directly influence federal legislators or government officials.

Those Awful Cold Calls

I spent several months and many hours networking in my quest to get a contract; one of my least-pleasant activities was making the dreaded cold calls. These are phone calls that one makes to a stranger seeking a meeting hoping for a meeting or even to be hired.

During one of my marketing calls, I was informed that a prestigious law firm might be looking for GR assistance in Washington. The firm was located on the 54th floor of a high-rise office building in Toronto with a beautiful view of Lake Ontario. A meeting was set. I was reminded often when making calls how helpful and friendly the Canadian business people were.

A distinguished-looking man welcomed me into his office. We spoke briefly before he asked me about my plans for my company; he was leaning back in his large brown leather chair, looking at my resume. I also handed him letters of recommendation, which he quickly reviewed. He complimented me on my experience.

He gave me a brief overview of the firm's priorities and their needs in Washington and then asked me how I thought I could help them. I knew that the firm had a robust energy practice and since I had been engaged with energy-related policies throughout most of my career, I thought that I would be a good fit.

"*Pathiclly ... pisifically ... pacificly.*" I stumbled over "specifically," I didn't know what to think other than "*Do I flee now or endure further embarrassment?*" Especially when I saw him rocking back and forth in his big leather chair. Back and forth. Back and forth.

I apologized and attempted to finish my thought saying that my energy background could be especially beneficial to their potential needs in Washington. I quickly tried to regain my composure. We talked for a few more minutes. I couldn't wait to get out of there. He graciously shook my hand, smiled, and wished me well.

I wasn't hired. I understood.

Time to move on. There were more calls to be made.

VOLUNTEERING AT CHRISTMAS

The first year I decided to stay in D.C., I vowed that I would not feel sorry for myself. I would find a food kitchen where I could help. I had always assumed that there was a need for volunteers, especially on holidays. I called several churches in downtown and the Capitol Hill area that were within a few miles from my house.

I quickly learned that waiting until the last minute to make calls, hoping to help serve those who had fallen on hard times, was not the right way to go. Those with whom I spoke said they didn't need any more help during the holidays, but noted that volunteers were always in demand apart from holidays.

After several unsuccessful calls, I heard the friendly voice of a church volunteer at a nearby Methodist church. She gave me directions and said that she would see me the following day.

Deep Breaths

As I walked across the parking lot, I noticed some crumbling red bricks. Discarded beer and soda cans were scattered near the entrance. I opened the heavy wooden door to the basement where the meals were being served. I asked a woman who looked in charge how I could help, offering to stand behind a long counter to dish out plates of food. That way, I wouldn't have to talk with the men, women, and children shuffling along the food line. I was nervous and sad at the same time. I was glad that I was there to help those in need, but I was very shy and unsure of what to say to them.

"Here's an apron in case you need it. Now go mingle with the crowd," an elderly, gray-haired lady smiled and gently directed me toward the long table.

Everyone seemed to be in a good mood, especially enjoying the turkey, mashed potatoes and gravy. Milk, white bread, and oranges were also popular.

I spotted a few hungry diners smacking their lips and scraping their forks to get the last bits. Some even quickly licked their plates. Others chatted with new friends. *Silent Night* and other Christmas carols played in the background. Several people sang along and tapped their feet.

I approached a table with the men and women plunging their forks into their meals. I asked them their names. Were they having a nice time? One of the women at the table had a small child with her. She had just sat down and cut some turkey into small bits to feed her daughter. I smiled at both of them and the mother smiled back. I asked them their names.

"This is my daughter, Ingrid. I'm Rosa."

Bit by bit, the little one was fed. Rosa waited patiently to take even one bite until her daughter was finished eating. She told me that she used to have a good job cleaning houses, but was now unemployed. She said that she struggled to feed her six-year-old daughter and that is why she was here at the church. She added that she was thankful for one warm meal but wished that she had a job.

I spotted some people snatching an extra orange or milk carton and sliding them into a plastic bag under the table. I told Rosa to take an extra orange. At first, she refused to take it, saying that someone else with a child would need it. I insisted and slid the two oranges into her bag.

"You like one? We can share."

"No, Rosa, but thank you." We hugged briefly.

When I walked out of the church several hours later, I thought about Rosa and others who were there just because they were down on their luck. I counted my blessings.

SLIPPING AWAY

TWO BIG MOVES:
SELLING THE FARM AND MOVING TO TOWN

Two years after my father died, my mother made the decision in 1984 to sell the farm and move from Reliance Road to a modest wooden house three miles away in Whitewater. She told me that it wasn't an easy decision for her to move away from Reliance Road, but she was relieved not to have to worry about all the farm-related responsibilities. Robert had recently begun working at a local bank as a trust administrator and helped with the sale.

Mother's house in Whitewater.

ONCE A TEACHER, ALWAYS A TEACHER

"Lots of memories. Good and not so good," my mother told me during one of my visits.

She also thought about giving up teaching after my father died, but said it still brought her enjoyment most of the time. She continued to teach for eleven years.

In recognition of 23 years of teaching, she was presented with a U.S. flag that was flown over the U.S. Capitol on the day of her retirement, May 5, 1983.

THE FLAG
OF THE
UNITED STATES
OF AMERICA

This is to certify that the accompanying flag was flown over the United States Capitol on May 5, 1983, at the request of the Honorable Beryl Anthony, Jr., Member of Congress.

This flag will be presented to Mrs. Margaret Winn on the occasion of her retirement from the teaching profession after 23 years.

George M. White, FAIA
Architect of the Capitol

21216

MOVING TO FAIRHAVEN ASSISTED LIVING

In 1986, my mother broke her hip after she slipped on a loose rug in her home in Whitewater. She had surgery at a Fort Atkinson hospital, a short, 20-minute drive away.

After a brief period of recuperation, she was moved to the skilled nursing and assisted living unit at Fairhaven in Whitewater to complete it.

Once she had recuperated fully, she moved into a small, sun-filled apartment overlooking a park in the independent living area at Fairhaven where she resided for three years until it was determined that she needed extra care due to her early-onset dementia.

At first, she wasn't very pleased about not being able to return to her home. However, my siblings and I believed that Mother should no longer live alone for the sake of her own safety. Before too long, she began to enjoy her cozy apartment and mingled with other residents, especially 92-year-old Vivian. They became very good friends and eventually became roommates.

My mother spent the rest of her life on the second floor in the skilled nursing unit until her death related to the dementia.

Author's Note: My mother remained at Fairhaven until her death at age 82. I will always be grateful for their kindness and care as she progressed from independent living to assisted living.

"THE FULL CATASTROPHE"

As I was writing this memoir, I thought about life and how it can break our hearts or bring us happiness. That's just the way life is sometimes. I was reminded of the story *Zorba the Greek* by Nikos Kazantzakis, when Zorba tells a young friend that he's *learned to embrace all of life: the joys, the sorrows, the full catastrophe.*

Bridge Games—Joys

Elizabeth, Martha, and my mother settled into their metal folding chairs to play bridge on a balmy Wisconsin June afternoon, while Jane locked her wheelchair in place.

The "girls" had been playing once a month for more than 20 years at one another's homes and had remained close friends, supporting each other through many happy, as well as difficult, times. Stories were swapped about their children, husbands, travels, and health as they sat around the card table. Political debates were off-limits, which was a good idea as my mother was the only Democrat; the others were staunch Republicans.

My mother loved to play bridge, especially after my father died. Playing with her good friends helped fill a void. After a few hands, the gals usually took a break.

Today, Mother was hosting. Coffee and lemon bars—everyone's favorite—were served.

"Here's milk if anyone needs it."

Jane said, laughing. "Oh, I remember the milk from the farm, Margaret. Our girls loved drinking it when we were visiting. So thick. They didn't like drinking the milk from the store after they tasted Jay's milk."

My mother piped up. "Well, you know when Kay broke her leg, we had to buy milk for her from the A&P; she wasn't drinking enough from our milk tank because she couldn't stand how thick it was. Of course, Jay hated the thought of us buying milk. You can imagine," Mother said, looking serious.

"Oh, my! I had no idea. Oh, I could just see Jay's reaction," Jane laughed.

Long, Warm Friendships

The women's friendship extended beyond the card table. I recalled my mother telling me about a confidential conversation she had with one of her bridge club friends years ago. The friend had come to talk to my mother about her daughter's upcoming wedding. The bride-to-be's father was refusing to attend because their daughter was marrying a Latino. Mother's friend didn't know what to do. My mother said that it was important for her to attend. The bride was her daughter, after all.

"You'll never regret going," my mother advised.

Mother's friend did attend the wedding, sitting in the back row.

Years later, I found out that several of my high school classmates had also confided in my mother. She always kept their secrets and gave light and warmth to all those who needed it.

Struggling for Words

On a bright Saturday morning, Mother called me in D.C. and asked all her usual questions: *Am I getting enough to eat? How's work? How's your social life? How's Doug?*

* * *

My Friend Doug

Doug and I worked separately in legislative affairs in the White House and on Capitol Hill, so we often met after work at Bullfeathers, a local watering hole, to unwind. During the summer months, we went sailing on his boat on the Chesapeake Bay. I wasn't much help with the actual details of sailing, but I was a reliable retriever of Bud Lites from the galley on hot days.

* * *

Mother always like to hear what I was up to. Of course, she shared how well (or not) she had played at the last bridge games.

Today, for the first time, I thought I detected hesitation as she grasped for the correct words.

"Sorry, I can't remember, can't remember the word I'm looking for." Her voice was tense.

"That's okay, Mother. Happens to me too."

"Yes, and I don't know why. Something's not right."

"Maybe you're just having an off day."

We didn't talk long that day. She was going to work in her garden.

"Good luck, Sweetie. Love you."

I hung up, very upset and alone. Even though I lived in D.C., my mother and I stayed connected by phone. Over the past several months, some conversations with her had been better than others. I wondered if she was showing signs of early dementia. Maybe she was depressed? *So what if she was forgetful?* I told myself.

I forgot words sometimes too. Maybe I was in denial.

Sorrows

When I got home from work late on a Friday afternoon, a message was waiting on my phone.

"Hello. It's Elizabeth. Please call me. It's about your mother." I listened to the message several times and detected an urgency in Elizabeth's voice. Dread washed over me.

I called her back and thanked for her caring so much about my mother. She told me about some of the changes that her bridge friends have observed in recent months.

"Her ability to play cards has been deteriorating noticeably. She doesn't want us to talk and visit at the card table. She gets very angry, even to the point of gritting her teeth. She puts down her cards and folds her arms across her chest. Sometimes she would even bark, 'Did we come here to talk or play cards?'" Elizabeth spoke softly.

I didn't know what to say in response to her words. She also said that my mother's minister told her that Margaret had begun to arrive at church at 11:00 AM on a Tuesday or Wednesday. She would quietly apologize when she was told that she had arrived on the wrong day. Then she would turn around and drive home.

How sad and frightening was that?

Elizabeth continued. "We have loved Margaret so much for so long. We just don't know what to do. You can imagine how terrible we all feel. We want to spare her any embarrassment and protect her dignity, but I feel it's up to me to let you know that we seem to be getting into a more and more difficult situation. We do not know in which direction to move."

My mother had always been a private person and one who respected others' privacy. Now, the minute she stepped out of her tidy house, she was slapped in the face with mistake after mistake—the wrong time, the wrong street, and wrong names.

I became alarmed and angry and struggled to keep panic at bay. I wept for my mother's future.

I didn't know if I was more panicked or depressed or both. Maybe just numb.

My poor mother. *She must be so scared.*

I had always thought I would be dealing with my parents' health-related issues while in my forties, surrounded by a husband and two kids. I guess not.

I had no choice but to head back to Wisconsin. I took a week off work and flew home.

Dinner at Mother's

Mother stood at the front door of her house, smiling and wiping her soapy hands on her blue gingham apron as I pulled into the driveway. The afternoon sun bounced off her auburn hair, which looked like it had been recently curled at Carol's Beauty Shop in Whitewater.

"Hello, Mother. How are you? Nice to see you. Your hair looks so pretty," I said, smiling broadly and giving her a big squeeze. I dropped my bags and followed her into the kitchen, tugging at the bow tied at the back of her apron.

"Do you remember the first apron I made to show at the Walworth County Fair sewing contest, Mother? Probably was the first thing I ever sewed. Pretty ugly, as I remember."

She chuckled.

Soap and Potatoes

I was completely taken aback to see her scrubbing potatoes in soap and water in the sink. She dipped the potatoes into the water and scrubbed again, then she laid them on the dish drainer to dry. She did the same for several more potatoes. She then cut them into quarter pieces.

"Mother, what are you doing? Why are you washing the potatoes with soap?" I asked, my voice rising even as I tried to chase the panic away.

"Well, what does it look like? I always do this!" I recognized the edgy tone in her voice and caught a quick look of anger flashing across her pale face.

"I thought I would make some potatoes and meatloaf for you. You've loved them since you were this high." She pointed to her waist. "Can I get you anything? There's Diet Sprite in the fridge. I'm not sure what else. Just help yourself. There's milk, of course."

I scanned a note that she had written and taped to the refrigerator door. "Supper for who? Kay. Potatoes. Do I have soap? Meatloaf. Dinner, pizza, and Kringle." I was particularly taken aback when I saw my business card on the door with "*Daughter*" written on the front in her tidy script. That stung.

COMPANY

Daughter

Kathleen J. Winn
Washington Representative

Suite 602
1155 15th Street N.W.
Washington, D.C. 20005

202/331-0212

Pizza Time

"Why don't you have a nice shower and I'll put the pizza in the oven. You can have a few potatoes on the side. I have raspberry Kringle too. I don't have any liquor. Well, no, I think I have some crème de menthe. Not sure how old it is."

"Let's have our dinner now, Mother, then I'll have a nice long shower," I responded.

We sat down at the dining room table, which was set with her fancy Royal Dalton dishes and good silverware. The pizza on the white ceramic platter was half its original size and looked like a hockey puck. Three pieces of raw potatoes were on a side plate.

"Here, Sweetie. I've nibbled most of the day. You go ahead. I'll have a banana and Kringle. Tell you the truth, I was never a real fan of pizza," she said, unfolding a paper napkin. I tried cutting the pizza, but it slipped across my plate. Somehow, I managed to cut it in two, picked up one half, and took a bite.

"Did I keep it in the oven too long? If it's too well done, I think I have another one," she said, beginning to get up from the table. I couldn't stop her from looking for another pizza. Instead of pizza from the freezer, she pulled out a chunk of moldy cheese that had expired two months previously.

I retrieved another Diet Sprite and headed to the den to sit on her tasteful, lemon-colored sofa.

On my way, I slipped the pizza into the trash bin, minus the three bites. I stared down at my soda can, slowing rubbing my index finger around the rim.

I looked at the piles of different magazines she had spread on the piano.

"Boy, Mother, you've got quite a collection of magazines here. Why so many? Looks like a dozen different ones," I remarked, sitting across from her on the sofa. "You don't read all them, do you?" I asked with a small dose of sarcasm.

"I don't have any vices, okay. They bring me pleasure. That's why. You know your mother has always been a reader. (*Really? None of us had time to read on the farm.*) You're welcome to look at any of them." There was that firm, angry tone again.

* * *

Time to Step Up

"Mother, you know that some of your friends are worried about you. I mean, a few of your close friends. Well, you know, they care about you and ..."

She sat more stiffly in her chair and pushed her coffee cup away.

"What are you trying to suggest? What do you mean?" she asked in a stern voice.

"Well, they're very worried about your forgetfulness. I am too, but we all have off days."

She sat motionless looking down at her dress, except to rub her right hand slowly along the top of her thigh. She stared directly at me. She sighed. The corners of her mouth fell.

"Well, then, I might as well be dead."

LUNCH AT THE COUNTRY KITCHEN

My mother loved going for car rides along her favorite winding country roads, looking at Holstein cows resting near the barbed wire fences and happily chewing their cuds. I wondered if she enjoyed the rides because they reminded her of life on our farm.

When I visited from D.C., we often stopped to have lunch at a local restaurant before heading back to Fairhaven. Today's destination was the Country Kitchen, a well-scrubbed restaurant with blond wood walls and bland plastic chairs. Salt and pepper shakers, mustard, ketchup, and saltine crackers were placed in the same order on all the tables.

"Welcome to Country Kitchen. Two of you? Please follow me." A young, perky teenaged waitress with a plastic name tag, Debbie, on the front of her blouse, handed us the laminated menus with a bright red barn and farm animals on the front. After a few minutes, she returned to take our order.

"I'll have a small house salad and the tuna fish salad sandwich. And coffee please. Black. Mother, you still want the chicken salad plate? That right?"

She nodded yes. "And just water," she said formally.

"Thank you, Debbie," I said.

"Oh, you're welcome. Not exactly booming here today. So, your orders should be here in no time." She smiled and turned back to the kitchen.

"Would you like a roll and some butter, Mother? The rolls are nice and warm." She took one roll and three pats of butter, but didn't eat any.

"Here you are." Debbie cheerfully gave me my house salad and coffee. I noticed Mother was frowning, and staring at my salad as I began to eat.

Just then Debbie walked by.

"What about me? Where's mine?" Mother barked. Debbie's eyes widened.

"It's OK, Mother. I ordered a salad first. Our sandwiches should be here soon. She hasn't forgotten. Want some of mine?"

"No, you eat."

The telltale muscles in her jaws were pulsing, always a sure sign of bewilderment and agitation. Just as quickly, she looked embarrassed and stared down at her lap.

After a short wait, the waitress delivered our food; we managed to get through the rest of lunch uneventfully. Mother didn't eat much of her sandwich, but she discreetly and quickly stuffed the rolls and butter in her purse.

As we left, I followed her and thanked Debbie.

"Sorry about that."

"Oh, no problem. I understand. You wouldn't believe some of the people I have to put up with. Don't even. Don't worry about it. Have a good one."

* * *

I was relieved that our trip back to Fairhaven was only a short 10-mile drive. I tuned the radio to a light classical station.

I thought maybe soothing music would provide some comfort. *I think we both need something calming.*

I was still upset by her outburst at lunch. My patience was becoming as fleeting as my mother's memory.

"Mother, why don't you give me those rolls and butter? They'll just get your purse dirty when the butter melts." My voice became increasingly firm as I reached for her purse.

Even today, I have no idea why I confronted her. I knew it was the disease that was slowly chipping away at her, but sometimes I became angry and shamefully, impatient. "Oh, just let me have them."

I'll recover them when we get back to her room, I told myself. *She probably wouldn't remember anyway.*

"We had a nice time, didn't we, Mother? I'll be back in the morning."

She nodded, opened her stained purse, and took out the rolls and butter.

Is she really going to take out those rolls and butter again? What is it with them?

She handed them to me.

"Here, for you."

Five Hundred Dollars!

My mother insisted on keeping her olive-green leather wallet with the snap top and a small yellow flower on the front close by in her room at Fairhaven. During one of my visits, I realized that it had been my favorite wallet during high school. Twenty years later and it reappeared!

"Mother, I remember this," as I rubbed the soft leather and snapped and unsnapped the clasp I used to do when I was a teenager.

As I did so, I found a pat of butter wrapped in a small paper napkin inside the wallet. The butter had soaked through the napkin and into the fabric. I told her I didn't think we needed to have the squares of butter in the wallet and I threw the pats away. I could tell that she wasn't pleased by her predictable set jaw.

I looked in the side where I used to keep my one-dollar bills, and saw a $500 fake bill. I pulled it out.

"Mother, you're rich! Five hundred dollars!" I proclaimed in a rather loud voice. Some may have called it irrational exuberance.

"Shut up! I don't want every one knowing my business!" She looked at me directly, leaned forward in her chair, and took the wallet. I have to admit that I was surprised and upset to hear her raise her voice and tell me to shut up. I was relieved to know that no one in the Fairhaven activity room was paying any attention; they were napping, talking to themselves, or chatting with their teddy bears.

"Mother, it's OK. It's not real money. No one is going to take it from you. Here, let's put it back where it's safe and sound."

"They don't know that!" she shouted.

Well, she does have a point, I thought to myself.

TIME PASSES

The bright sun splashed across the flat, frozen fields of southern Wisconsin, which glistened like glazed crystal. I was driving a Ford Mustang rental along Highway 12 from the Milwaukee airport to Whitewater to visit my mother at her house prior to moving her to Fairhaven. The stubbly rows of harvested corn stalks reminded me of the buzz cuts the boys had worn in my high school class.

I looked across a field and saw a lone farmer spreading a load of manure, his dog trotting alongside the tractor. It reminded me of those times sitting on our old Case tractor doing just that same thing. It was a job I hated, especially when the wind suddenly changed direction and the nasty stuff headed my way.

Passing the turn-off for Reliance Road, I slowed down to look at our old farm from the highway. The once bright red barn was now a faded pink; the long, white wooden fences that had ringed the property were gone, replaced with sagging wire. Tree limbs were stripped bare from passing storms. I thought about growing up here decades ago.

Maybe we don't forget the places where we began as children. Was I feeling nostalgic? Or depressed by years gone by?

In an odd way, I was also comforted. I still felt a strong connection to the place I had left 25 years ago. I recalled the happy hours playing with Sissie, walking along Reliance

Road on summer nights, chasing fireflies, or listening to the crickets and the muffled noise of the semis on Highway 12 two fields away.

As I drove, more memories washed through me. Despite the occasional painful or unhappy events, my childhood had been a good one.

TUSSLE ON THE SECOND FLOOR

Imagine my surprise as I stepped out of the Fairhaven elevator and saw my mother and her neighbor entwined rolling on the hallway floor in front of their adjoining rooms.

Something's definitely not right. Tippy, the resident black lab with white on the tip of his tail, always heads to a room when he hears someone in distress. Most of the time, he would beat the nurses to the room. He was a reliable four-legged alert system! Tippy was already waiting at the door when a nurse rushed over to my mother and Martha, both tugging and pushing each other.

I leaned down and asked my mother if she was in any pain. She was shaking. I could tell by the way she looked up at me that she was upset or maybe angry or both. One of her blue slippers was nearby on the floor. She was clutching her favorite plastic red, yellow, and blue necklaces. I helped her to sit up, hoping that she would calm down.

Joan, the nurse for this floor, gently helped Martha, a petite, frail lady with beautiful white hair, sit up on her bed.

"Ladies, do you hurt anywhere? Margaret? How about you, Martha?" Joan sounded alarmed. Martha was whimpering.

"Ladies, to be on the safe side, I am going to call our doctor and ask him to take a good look at you. He is going to want to hear about your fight. What was it about?"

After probing for answers, it turned out that my mother had gone into Martha's apartment, believing it was hers. My mother was adamant. So she tackled Martha and told her to get out of "my" room. Thus the fight began.

A STUBBORN DANE

Picture your mother strutting down a hallway in her favorite red high heels, carrying a walker over her head and smiling broadly. This visual stuck in my head as I arrived at Fairhaven. Joan, one of her regular nurses, had briefly mentioned in a recent phone call to remind her to tell me something about my mother and her walker.

The day before, I had flown from Washington D.C. and drove to Whitewater to take over for my sister, who had to go back to work in New Jersey.

My mother had broken her leg a week earlier. My anxiety level always spiked when I went to visit her, as she was showing more advanced signs of dementia. Now, her broken leg added to my worry.

"How's she doing?" I asked Joan, who was dispensing meds near the front lobby.

"She struggles with using her walker, but she's making progress. She's sharper some days than others, and lately she's been pretty with it. Doing well, all things considered. The meds are keeping her pain at a minimum. We know she's a fighter." Joan grinned. "She's bounced back pretty fast physically."

She continued. "When I reminded Margaret to use her walker, she frowned. Her jaw set. Hand on her hip. She spun around and gave me a real nasty look."

"Maybe it's the stubborn Dane in her," I suggested.

"We watched Margaret head back to her room. Know what she did? Wasn't more than a couple of minutes. Well, wouldn't you know, here she comes down the hall, carrying the walker over her head! Still trotting toward us in her red high heels."

" 'Here. You want it? ' Margaret asked, like a little kid."

"We had all we could do not to laugh. She's such a doll. Oh, we had a chuckle over that."

"Thank you. I'll go find her now," I said.

And when I did, I said, "Hello, Mother! Nice to see you. You're looking good. New dress?"

She smiled and did a little curtsy, even holding on to the walker.

FOUR OF CLUBS

I gently untied the faded blue terry-cloth bib from the back of my mother's neck and draped it over her wheelchair. Supper was finished; the staff had cleared away the Styrofoam cups and plastic utensils. Nurses began their nightly rounds.

Those interested in playing Pokeno, a board game similar to Bingo, slowly shuffled to a nearby room reserved for games. Some residents struggled more than others. Bertha, one of the residents, was trying desperately to free her walker from a wheelchair blocking her path.

"What's wrong here? You're in my way." she grunted to no one in particular.

Her outburst woke Vivian, who stared at her.

"You're on the wrong street, Honey," Vivian grinned as she helped Bertha untangle my mother's wheelchair.

I wheeled my mother next to Vivian. She was lucky to have had the cheerful and loving Vivian as her friend and roommate for seven years. I didn't know if she was fully aware of my mother's fuzziness, but she was always sweet to her even though she did have her own moments of confusion.

"Mother, we're going to play Pokeno. Maybe we'll get lucky and win something." She leaned toward me and tried to say something, but I couldn't understand her garbled words, which were trapped inside her. She then stared off in the distance. It broke my heart.

I looked at the mother I had always loved: a proud woman who was being torn apart piece by piece by her dementia. The one constant was that she was my mother—no one could take that away. Who would have guessed that she was a mother of three, had received a master's degree after her children had grown, taught home economics for more than 20 years, was an ace cook, and a confidante to many?

"Well, Mother, the game will be starting soon. Let's see if we can win, okay?"

Wheelchairs and walkers were locked in place at the wooden table. Early evening amber light cast a warm glow over the room.

Some, like Vivian, were catching a last-minute snooze; others were staring at no one in particular. Gladys held a teddy bear tightly, making sure the bear didn't get snatched away. Clair, a World War I survivor, was tapping his cane impatiently. The wait was over when Wendy, a staff member in charge of activities, arrived and checked each player's board, making sure that everyone had what they needed.

As Wendy was preparing for the card game, sweet and timid Ken smiled at me. I had a soft spot for him and walked over to his side of the table to say a quick hello.

"How are you today, Ken?" He was looking forlorn.

"I didn't know that I had sat on a wet towel. When I got up, I thought I'd lost my youth," he said in his soft-spoken voice.

"Well, I'm glad that you're okay and you're here to play." I gave him a quick hug.

It's Game Time!

"Everybody ready to win? Let's play," Wendy spoke loudly and slowly.

Wendy held up a huge Ace of Spades card, and rotated it so all could see. She repeated slowly, "Ace of Spades. Ace of Spades." Each player had a board with small replicas of playing cards on them. If players had a picture of that card on their board, they would put a chip on it. When a player had a string of chips, as in Bingo, he or she would call out, "Pokeno!"

It wasn't long before Ken squinted at Wendy, saying, "What's that again?"

"Ace of Spades."

"Alright," he said softly and flashed a warm, closed-lipped smile.

Gladys, next to him, tried to be helpful, looking at his board.

"You don't have it."

He smiled and said, "What's that?"

Gladys' voice rose. "YOU DON'T HAVE IT!"

"Alright."

My mother was still rubbing the top of the Formica table with two red chips. Very intently, she leaned forward extending her arm as far as it could go, and then slid the chips back again. Her movements were like those that I had seen her do so many times rolling out dough for her Danish rolls.

Suddenly, I motioned to Wendy that a woman in a lounge chair along the side of the room looked distraught. Wendy asked me take over while she tended to the situation.

"Sure." *Nothing complicated*, I told myself.

Piece of Cake—or so I Thought

All heads turned toward me as I announced loudly and crisply. "Alright, everyone ready? Here we go. We have an Eight of Diamonds. Eight of Diamonds." I continued to rotate around the group with the large card. I quickly glanced at my mother, who was still moving her chips, intently focused on her task.

So far, so good, but no winners yet.

Pokeno—Serious Business

Of course, some of the residents were more focused than others. A few looked out for the people next to them, trying to be helpful. Others, like Gladys, always inspected her neighbors' boards for cheating, and was more than ready to blow the whistle. A few nodded off, chips gradually slipping from their hands onto their laps, or rolling onto the floor.

My next round, I repeated "Four of Spades. Four of Spades," moving the card from left to right. All of a sudden, Gladys belted out, "That's not a Four of Spades. That's a Four of Clubs!"

"You're absolutely right, Gladys! Okay, everyone. We have a Four of Clubs. A Four of Clubs," I said, attempting a quick recovery. *How embarrassing!*

Clair shouted, "Where did you come from? Who are you anyway?"

"I don't know. She must be a girl. She's got a skirt on," said Bertha, who had a touch of bulldog in her looks with her perpetually pinched mouth and plunging forehead. She pushed back her wheelchair from the table in disgust. "Get rid of her. *GET RID OF HER!*"

Thankfully, Wendy returned to take over. "Everyone ready for one more game?" Wendy smiled as she began. "Here we go. Nine of Clubs. Nine of Clubs."

In a few minutes, Gladys won. "Pokeno," she bellowed. The players began a slow caravan to their rooms after Gladys received a banana for her prize.

"Well, Mother, I don't know about you, but I'm tired. What'd you say we head for bed?"

She clung to my hand as I walked slowly behind the wheelchair, moving it toward her darkened room, I remembered her words when we were children: *"Sleep tight. Don't let the bedbugs bite, but if they do, take off your shoe and kick them 'til they're black and blue."*

I kissed her hollow, soft cheek, turned away, and left her until the morning. I wondered, as I often did, *Why. Why her? Why me?*

This never gets easier.

A BELOVED TEACHER

Many members of the Fairhaven staff had had my mother as a teacher. Often, when I arrived, they would give me something they made in my mother's classes: a strawberry pin cushion, a chicken casserole recipe, a cotton apron. One mother said her son still talked about learning how to sew on a button or boil an egg when the boys in shop and the girls in home economics switched places for a semester. My mother wanted the boys to learn some basics. The heartwarming stories from staff lifted my spirits. Hearing stories about some humorous things that Mother did also helped ease my sadness.

HERE COMES VIVIAN!

While Mother was having her usual afternoon nap, I visited with Joan and Mary, one of the other nurses. They updated me in more detail about Mother's overall health and told me who had died and news of other goings-on. Whitewater was a small town so there were few secrets.

Out of the corner of my eye, I spotted Vivian heading toward us. The two seniors had some kind of special bond. They often told each other how much they loved each other.

"Hello, Vivian! Nice to see you!" I greeted her.

She grinned from ear to ear. I didn't know if she remembered me from earlier visits, but that didn't matter.

"What's going on here? Nobody died, did they?"

"Oh no, Vivian, no one died. We're just chatting about Margaret and how well she's doing with her broken leg." Mary rubbed Vivian's back.

"Okay then." She turned and shuffled down the hall, leaning forward over her walker as if she were facing a 30-mile-per- hour wind.

"They're a perfect match. She can be quite funny, just like your mother. They keep us on our feet!" Mary smiled, leaning against the wall.

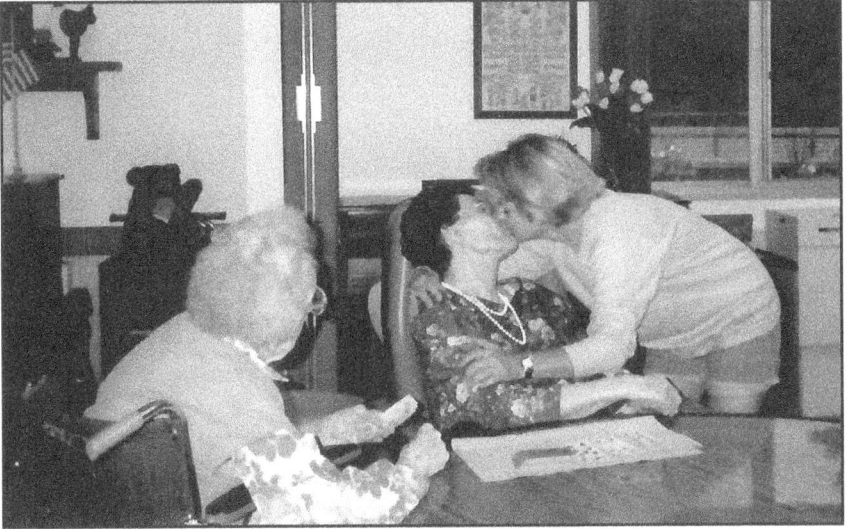

Vivian, my mother, and me at Fairhaven.

THE RED BUTTON

Mother's spunkiness reminded me of another conversation she had with a nurse when she was recovering from hip surgery in Madison. The nurse was checking her vitals before bedtime and related this story to me at that time.

"Now, one last item, Margaret. Remember we talked about what you need to do if you have to go to the bathroom. What do you have to do?"

Mother stuck her jaw out, looked straight at the nurse, and gave her a steely look.

"Well, I do what I always do. Get up and go."

"No, Margaret. See the red button here. Press that. Someone will come to help. You have to keep off your feet for a few days."

"Oh, good night!"

That was my mother's way of saying, "Get out of my face."

THE FIRST GLANCE

Whenever I visited Fairhaven, the first glance at my mother was always the hardest. The toll from her dementia had left her lively, brown eyes milky, often frozen in some distant place. Her hands, as usual, were clasped together, fingers firmly entwined. Her chin was resting on her hands.

I gingerly made my way around a tangle of wheelchairs and walkers. I greeted her with as cheery a voice as I could muster. She was easy to spot in the activity room, sitting quietly in her wheelchair, making no strange or unseemly noises. "Hello, Mother. So nice to see you. It's me, Kay, your daughter. How are you today?" I bent down and kissed her. I smiled. Smiles were always important.

She stared at me with a puzzled, "Do I know you?" expression. I waited for her to smile or give me some other form of recognition. *Does she know me? Is she in any pain?*

I looked at the maze of veins in her hands as I gently stroked them. They were soft and warm, still straight, masking years of hard work on our dairy farm. All those pails of milk she carried, all those weeds pulled, all those bales of hay lifted, Danish rolls baked, and roasts and potatoes cooked. All those dishes washed, both on the farm and after cooking demonstrations for her home economic students at Franklin Junior High School.

Soon, a smile slowly spread from ear to ear. She began vigorously rubbing my arm back and forth, back and forth. Whomever she thought I was, she seemed to like me.

That was all that mattered.

FULL CIRCLE

I stood in the baking aisle at the local Walmart wondering if my mother would have any interest in playing with the plastic measuring spoons and small glass bowls. Would seeing them bring back memories of all those hours she spent cooking three meals a day for the family? Given her dementia, would she even realize what the spoons were used for?

You never know, I told myself.

I put two different sized bowls and the measuring spoons in my shopping cart.

Then I walked to the baby section too to pick out a couple of bibs. Mother's were looking worn and it was time for new ones. Her favorite color was blue, so I found two with pretty blue and yellow flowers and added them to my shopping cart. I heard that plastic spoons made feeding babies easier. If it's easier for babies, it should be for my mother. I put them in my cart too.

With her blank stare, I thought, *"Maybe she's thinking about the times I sat with her in the front seat when she drove our white Oldsmobile into town. She knew I loved to be with her, especially when we held hands walking down Main Street to the IGA to buy groceries and the shoe store so I could get a new pair of saddle shoes."*

If I could ever get over my inability to feed her, I would use the plastic spoons. At the moment, I didn't have the fortitude to feed her or watch as an attentive staff member slowly slid a spoonful of something I couldn't identify into her mouth. Often, Mother turned her head away from her plate or got distracted, and some of her meal would slide down her bib.

I don't remember the point I felt that I could feed my mother. I think it was around the time that she was still struggling to remember me. Whoever she thought I was, she was very receptive to my feeding her.

Quickly, I looked around the activities room. Heads nodded around the table as the residents excitedly plunged spoons into bowls, pushed what looked like meatloaf around their plates, and sipped milk with two hands. The skimpiness of the meals seemed just enough to sustain sedentary lives.

I told my mother I would be back after she finished supper. Often, while we shuffled the cards around, we pretended to play Solitaire. I said silly things, or the same things over and over, especially telling her how much I loved her. Sometimes, she laughed or tried to speak before the words were clamped down. Anytime she laughed, I was hopeful that even fleetingly, she had some moments of contentment and happiness.

I wondered if I had ever known her when she was well. Had I tried hard enough or taken the time to really get to know her? Do we ever really know the people we love?

CARE CONFERENCE

My mother looked at nothing in particular. She had that same haunted, vacant look she had for several years. She and I were sitting at a long conference table waiting for her quarterly progress assessment. The head nurse, dietician, activities person, and social worker were seated around the table.

Mother's chin rested on her tightly entwined hands, her elbows resting on the arms of the wheelchair. She was napping as I gently rubbed her back.

Pam, the dietician, started the review. "Margaret is enjoying her 1,500-calorie reduction. Her weight is 168 pounds, which is a five-pound weight loss since November. Each food item continues to be served individually so she doesn't become frustrated with too many selections."

"Margaret's placement in small-group situations is monitored closely. Recently, her behavior has been very stable. Her behavior and involvement vary depending on the activity, but your mother enjoys her wood/block sorting task. It keeps her hands busy," Mary said, smiling at Mother.

Seated at the opposite end of the table, Carolyn, the head nurse, looked directly at me. She was a large woman with cropped black hair. "Margaret's Serentil, her medication for agitation, has been discontinued due to possible "pseudo-Parkinson" tremors. Since that was stopped three weeks ago, her tremors have lessened. Her bowels are normal."

Mother would be mortified. Bowels were her business.

Then Carolyn leaned forward, looking at directly at me.

"We were wondering, you know, how your mother would react when Vivian died. Did she show any signs of missing her good friend?"

Suddenly, Mother opened her eyes, leaned forward, and stared directly at Carolyn. Then she turned to me, looking frightened. I leaned over and hugged her, suppressing an irrational urge to erupt in laughter.

"It's okay, Mother. I love you. Everything'll be all right." I felt very sad and startled. Very shortly, Mother's face relaxed again and she began to doze.

I'll never forget that moment, witnessing my mother's reaction. It's very likely that it was the first time she actually heard those words mentioned out loud. "... when Vivian died."

Was I still rationalizing? No, I don't think so. When Vivian's body was removed from their room, no one said, "Margaret, say goodbye to Vivian. Vivian's dead," as they wheeled the small body out of the room. I was convinced that my mother's reaction during the review showed that it was highly unlikely that she missed Vivian until she heard the actual words "Vivian's dead."

* * *

The warmth and affection my mother and Vivian shared over five years were evidenced through smiles, soft touches, and hand-holding. As time passed and Mother's dementia worsened, these little signals replaced words. They had their own language.

"Oh, we love each other so, don't we, Honey!" Vivian said, smiling at Mother. Sometimes, a faint smile appeared on Mother's gaunt face. Sometimes, she tried to speak, but her words were garbled.

NO MORE MAGIC

In 1998, my mother's physical condition began to unravel; her ghost-like face and withered body finally began to collapse under the weight of her disease. Now, nothing was spared from its hideous grip. The enormity of my heartache increased in proportion to her deterioration. Her once-beautiful brown eyes became black pools. A thin layer of white flesh stretched over her protruding cheek bones. Her once-proud shoulders slumped forward as if one of the large rocks we had picked up on the farm was lodged on her back.

She was a proud and proper woman who had turned into a shell of her former self. It was like watching a Polaroid photo develop in reverse. Her memory had slowly faded into blackness. I felt despair at the loss of the mother I once knew.

STILL MY MOTHER

There were times that I admit I got angry at the person my mother had become, but the one constant was that she was still my bleary-eyed, jaw-gnashing mother. In our own way, we stayed connected. She liked playing pretend Bingo as we shuffled our chips around the board. Every now and then, I would say "Bingo!" Sometimes she looked at me briefly and smiled; other times, she just carried on moving her chips.

So Many Questions

Watching her personality gradually wither under the burden of bafflement and fear was very difficult. I often wondered if she was suffering from depression. Maybe she had been depressed for a long time. All her life? Did she have early-onset Alzheimer's, most likely, or had she suffered a series of mini-strokes?

"IT'S OK, MOTHER."

I was jogging on the Mall in Washington D.C. one chilly November day and realized that I had never told my mother it was "okay to go." She was rapidly declining physically and mentally. her dementia slowly eating away at her. Gone were the days when she was able to enjoy even simple pleasures of the day, such as seeing spring again, or snow. There were to be no more car rides on country roads when I came back to Whitewater for a visit.

I had flown in from D.C. and rented a car at the Milwaukee airport. After arriving at Fairhaven, I shared with Joan my intentions to tell my mother it was OK to go. Joan was a nurse who had been tending to my mother for several years. She told me that my mother had been through so much and that I was doing the right thing. She also told me how much the staff loved my mother as Joan wheeled her into a small waiting room. I looked up at the wall-mounted TV, reached for the remote, and turned down the volume. Of course, if it's a Sunday in November in Wisconsin, it's Packer time.

"Hello, Mother. Nice to see you! That's a pretty dress you have on," I said in as cheerful a voice as I could muster. She stared at the ceiling. I wiped saliva off the side of her mouth with a tissue. Her eyes were milky, her beautiful brown eyes long gone. She said nothing.

I cleared my throat and held her frail, soft hand, continuing to talk to keep from crying.

"Mother, I want to tell you something. I love you very much; we always told each other that we would fight for each other, didn't we?"

You can do this, I told myself. Deep breaths.

"I want you to know that it's okay to go, to be with Dad and your mother and father. I'll be alright, but, of course, I'll miss you."

Her face looked so peaceful, no frowning, no grinding of teeth. Now her hands were crossed on her chest. She dropped off into a deep sleep, her breaths seeming to come from somewhere deep inside.

Hope she's not comatose!

"Mother, I want to tell you again that it's okay to go. I'll be alright." I gently took her hands. Each time, I spoke louder, but no response.

"Mother! Mother! Time to get up. Up we go!"

She can't be dying!

I called out to Joan, who was walking past the room to dispense pills.

"Help me please. She's ... I think my mother may be dying. I told her it was okay for her to go, but I didn't mean right now!" I fought back tears.

"She does look so peaceful. Margaret! Wake up, Margaret." Joan's voice rose as she gently shook my mother's shoulder. "Margaret!" I sensed alarm. Again, "Margaret!"

Finally, my mother's eyes opened. Joan smiled at her, "That was some snooze you had. Well, you enjoy the rest of the afternoon with your daughter."

In a shaky voice, I said, "Thank you. I was getting very frightened! I was just trying to ease her passage, not persuade her to die right now."

The scare was over. I felt enormous relief. Then I wondered if I had done the right thing. She looked so peaceful and her breathing was so deep.

Had she heard my words? Had they brought her peace? I'll never know.

I looked into her eyes again and repeated my words.

"It's okay to go, Mother. I'll be alright. And, as always, I love you."

WHEN STILLNESS ARRIVES

My mother looked so peaceful in her coffin, surrounded by white lilies, her favorite flowers.

Oddly, for the first time in years, she looked like I remembered her when she was healthy and just napping. Her stillness was a stark contrast to my memories of her grinding her teeth until saliva and blood oozed from the side of her mouth. Her once-beautiful brown eyes had become milky, often frozen staring in some distant place. The illness had slowly chipped away at her brain.

I peered at her pale face, her fine eyelashes, the scar on her forehead, and her sealed lips. Her hair had been nicely styled by Janet from Janet's Salon. A blue necklace lay neatly on top of her favorite dress, a fuchsia, blue, and green dress. Nothing fancy, just a sensible dress that always looked nice on her. I kissed her cold lips and whispered "Goodbye, Mother." *Why did I whisper?* Maybe so she could finally rest in peace.

The smell of the lilies made me sick to my stomach and brought back memories of my father's funeral in this chapel 27 years ago. I quickly headed to a nearby bathroom and promptly threw up, relieved that no one else was there. I wiped tears from my face with a cool paper towel, and made sure that my mascara had not smeared.

I headed back to my sister's side and joined her in greeting our mother's friends as they slowly shuffled into the chapel. My brother was standing away from the entrance to the chapel, smoking a cigarette, talking with a couple of men I didn't know. They were laughing. Maybe Robert had told one of his favorite jokes. He was a good storyteller.

I was heartened by the kind words of those passing by.

"She was such a kind friend."

"So sorry. We all loved Margaret."

"She suffered so much. Now she's at peace."

"She was a doll."

"She was a match to Martha Stewart."

Several on my mother's former students expressed their sadness. "We had Mrs. Winn for home ec. She was always so friendly and helpful. We're sorry."

Those paying their respects reflected important aspects of my mother's life: students, faculty from the junior high school where she taught home economics, church friends, professors from the local college, bridge club friends, travel companions and last, but not least, her family. In addition to her three children, her sister, nieces, nephews, and grandchildren were here to celebrate Mother's eternal life.

The last of the mourners settled into their pews. From my seat near the minister, I noticed that several of my mother's bridge club friends sat with their heads bowed. I watched them wipe their eyes.

The July sun shone through the stained glass windows, casting brilliant reds and blues across the chapel.

The minister's wife stopped the organ music as the minister approached the dais. He greeted the congregation, offering words of comfort. We sang *Rock of Ages* and *Amazing Grace*. A soloist choir member sang *On Eagle's Wings*. Two grandchildren read Scripture and the gospel. The minister offered a brief meditation.

I tried to control my bad case of nerves. It was my turn to speak.

MY MOTHER'S EULOGY
DELIVERED JULY 12, 1999

"Dear Mother. Your long and difficult struggle—the burden of fear, bafflement and grief—has been silenced. Everything that you had imagined, learned and loved was slowly torn from you (and us) piece by piece. Yet, even as your illness continued to pull you down, you fought back with unfailing courage, strength, and most of all, dignity.

This is the mother, the sister, the grandmother of Maggie, Derek, Jayne, Blair, Marni, Jim, and Rog, the friend, and the teacher I want to cheer and salute today. Because through those very qualities that sustained you in sickness and in health, you have enriched the lives of many others.

Mother, I stand here today with tremendous sadness, but also with the knowledge that you're in a better place. Finally, it's your turn to smile, laugh, and bounce high. Eat all the vanilla ice cream that you want. (With any luck, there are no more cows to milk or dinners to cook.) Go ahead! Dance that stately minuet—better yet, dance that Charleston in those high heels. We can't forget those red high heels that you loved and insisted on wearing—even after you had your hip replaced a week earlier. I believe you would have called that "the stubborn Dane" in you.

I realize these words are my own, but I hope to capture the essence of you. I also want to reflect Diane and Robert's feelings. As I thought about what to say today, many words and thoughts floated around in my mind. I finally realized that much of it is found in the values you worked to instill in

Diane, Robert, and me. Now maybe we haven't kept a 100 percent track record – at least speaking for myself – but you planted the seeds. You got the basic lessons of life right, and because you did, you cast a long shadow. You lived and lead by example.

Some of the things that you taught us were to:

- Be honest in our day-to-day lives. We learned that early. I'm sure that Jayne and Maggie can vouch for this. When their desire to win playing cards was sometimes more important than playing by the rules, you set them straight quickly. No cheating.
- Try to treat others with respect and to appreciate their differing views.
- Never let integrity leave our side in our business dealings.
- Be a good listener—As you said so many times, "Sweetie, people love to talk about themselves. Just let them talk. You'll always find out a lot about them." I *know* that your friends trusted you. I *know* that your friends knew you kept your word.
- Be kind to others and be there for friends and those in need.

Of course, there are things that I'll especially remember: "Drink your milk." "No means no." "What do you care what other people think anyway?"

I guess it was Dad who ingrained in us that we were and always were to be good Democrats. I believe that the first things I learned were: my name, telephone number, and how to spell D-E-M-O-C-R-A-T. I may have the order mixed up.

You always fought to keep bitterness, anger and resentment at bay. You looked them in the eyes and did not flinch.

Essentially, you made the best of the hand you were dealt in life. For Midwesterners, this means no whining.

You were also a fighter and your own person – an early supporter of the Equal Rights Amendment – one of a handful in town. And, you drove 55-miles-per-hour, saying that it was more fuel efficient. This was in the early 1960s, no less.

At a family dinner last night, we shared some vanilla ice cream for dessert. After my niece, Marni, had a spoonful; I asked her how it tasted. She said to me, "I really don't eat vanilla ice cream. I just wanted to have a spoonful for Grandma."

I would like to read from the New Testament, Timothy: 4:6-9

The time has come for me to be gone.
I have fought the good fight to the end;
I have run the race to the finish:
I have kept the faith;
All there is to come now is the
crown of righteousness reserved for me.
Which the Lord, the righteous judge,
will give me on that Day; and not only to me
but to all those who have loved his appearing.

Let us join with one another in praying to God, not only for our mother, sister, grandmother, friend, and teacher, but also for peace and tolerance in the world, and for ourselves.

That those who bear the cross of pain in mind or body may never feel forsaken by God. For all those with whom our mother interacted – her many students and all those others – that they may continue to use and develop the gifts they have received through her. For the many friends she guided through life, may they keep her friendship alive by proclaiming her zest for life in all that they do.

May her vibrant spirit of generosity, strength, warmth, and love be an inspiration to us all.

Amen.

* * *

TURN LEFT TO ROOM 204

I took a deep breath, pushed the second-floor elevator button and turned left down the hall to my mother's room, Room 204. Even after ten years of coming here to visit her, I never knew what to expect as dementia slowly ate away at her frail body. This was the room in which I had spent hours holding her hand and telling her how much I loved her. We played pretend Solitaire, just shuffling cards.

When she seemed well enough during my visits from D.C., I would take her for car rides. She always seemed to enjoy those as she stared out the window looking at the fluffy clouds and blue skies. Her foot often tapped—always a good sign that she was in a good mood.

On this day, my mother wasn't sleeping in her single bed or sitting in her wheelchair in the nearby activity room, staring at nothing in particular, napping, or being fed by staff.

She had died three days ago.

Joan, the head nurse, spotted me and stopped dispensing pills to give me a big hug.

"We're all so sorry around here about your mother. She was such a kind lady. It was terrible that she suffered with her dementia for so long. We all loved her." She told me that if I needed anything when I was cleaning out my mother's room to give her a shout.

Three cotton dresses hung limply in the closet. A large poster of two puppies was taped on the ceiling above her bed.

I sat on the edge of my mother's bed as I looked around. Sadness swept through me. The room was stuffy and had an unpleasant odor.

Her Room—What Remained

Mother's environment had been reduced to sleeping in a single bed in a room with one small closet. It also contained a drawer full of Depends and some worn underwear. Her favorite red high heels were tucked safely away. Her wedding ring had long ago been removed. Her Bible lay on top of her drawer beside old church bulletins that her Methodist friends left behind. A flimsy blue curtain hung between her and Vivian.

It was also the room where she occasionally laughed at nothing in particular. When cheerfulness blessedly caressed her, she would slide her feet back and forth on the foot-rest on her wheelchair or tap them to the music of Lawrence Welk. Another favorite melody was, *Take Me Out to the Ball Game*. This was always a heart-warming sight.

* * *

"How are you doing?" Rita, one of the staff, poked her head in the room as I was about to sort the few items left. She leaned on her mop and cleaning cart.

"Your mother was such a nice lady," Rita said. "I know how much you loved her. All your visits from out East. This must be hard."

Tears welled up in her eyes, small streams meandering down her thin face; she wiped them away with the back of her red hand.

"Thanks to you and others who always helped me make my visits more bearable. I know she was loved, especially by staff here who had her as a teacher."

As Rita turned down the hall, pushing her cart, I wished that I could be more talkative; she was so empathic. I remembered something that my mother said to me shortly after my father died. "The trouble with sadness is that is that it seldom produces anything new to say."

As I was finishing packing the last of my mother's belongings, Joan came by. "I just wanted to see if you still needed anything. You know, we lost four just this week. Must be some record. Your mother, Mrs. Humphries ... let's see, Alice Green, and Bill Weston. Isn't that something?" she whispered.

"Well, that is something."

I wasn't sure what else to say.

AFTERWORD

What a trip down Memory Lane—or rather, Reliance Road— writing this book has been. From farmgirl roots to working in the White House and establishing my own successful government relations consulting firm focused on energy policy, I have lived a full and worthwhile life.

I encourage you to speak with relatives and friends to help you draw the picture of your life—not only for your sake, but for that of younger generations to come. I cherish the time spent with my family, especially those precious moments with my mother. It was because of her that I proudly walked down Reliance Road—independent, capable, and respected.

Thank you for taking the time to read this memoir. Perhaps it has also inspired you to write your own story. While you can, capture those memories. I am grateful to those who saved the letters, photos, and mementos that allowed me to pull the pieces together.

While writing this book, I reflected on the people, places, and events I hadn't thought about for a long time. I was reminded of the many things I had learned along the way. There were moments of joy, profound sadness, disappointment, surprises, and fears. I grew to understand the importance of capturing memories and the roles they play in our lives. My hope has been to inspire curiosity regarding the memories and how they change us over time. My mother's words, "Write, Sweetie, write!" have followed me throughout my career.

ACKNOWLEDGMENTS

Corinne Bradshaw

I am forever grateful to Corinne Bradshaw, my devoted spouse, who showed incredible patience, unwavering support, love, and generosity of her time. She made this journey easier by providing moments of side-splitting laughter during those times of my frustration, burnout, and lack of confidence. She was also my "IT" department, often solving problems when I panicked as I struggled with "technology" issues.

Family

I am ever grateful to my wonderful family members, who shared memories of life on the farm, many of which I had never heard before. They also helped me to create stories that brought the past to life.

To update the reader, after my loyal sister Diane graduated from UW–Whitewater, she pursued her interest in teaching art education. She also developed art programs for an elementary school in a Chicago suburb while earning her master's degree at Northern Illinois University. After several years of teaching, Diane married Roger, a businessman who traveled internationally. They had two daughters, Maggie and Jayne.

My brother Robert married Karen, a high school home economics teacher after he graduated from UW–Madison and began working as a trust officer at a local Janesville bank. It wasn't long before he established his own successful real estate and appraisal business, Winn Realty. Robert and Karen had three children: Marni, Derek, and Blair, who took over Winn Realty when Robert died after a brief illness in 2006.

205

It has been a joy watching my nieces and nephews and their children grow up. They are all kind, respectful, hardworking, whip smart, and well-grounded.

Friends & Readers

Many thanks to Katherine M. Bell, Mary Blayney, Doug Frost, Suzanne Kiraly, Cheryl Place, Larry Sommers, and Marti Thomas, who took the time to read my manuscript and offer critical feedback and inspiration. My sincerest gratitude to my friends who kindly listened to me talk endlessly about "the book," and offered words of support and encouragement.

I also want to thank Alice Engling, my mother's loyal, special angel.

Kira Henschel

I was very fortunate to have Googled "Editors in Wisconsin" after searching unsuccessfully for a year for an editor in the Washington, D.C. area where I lived. I realized when I was jogging one afternoon in early 2023 that most of my stories take place in Wisconsin; Kira's publishing and editing company—HenschelHAUS—was in Milwaukee. A bonus was that most of my family live in the Wisconsin area. We Zoomed. Kira explained her business and asked me what I had in mind for any next steps. "Write a book, I guess." I got lucky. We went to work.

Kira was a skilled listener and offered critical guidance, as well as words of encouragement, building my confidence. She helped me focus and let me write at my own pace. There were plenty of times that I thought about giving up, rather than pretending I had anything to say. She rescued me from the numerous rabbit holes I tumbled down while organizing the chapters of my life to create *Reliance Road*.

ABOUT THE AUTHOR

After 25 years of owning her own government relations consulting business, Kate (Kay) retired and has been enjoying life living in southern Maryland on a cliff above the Chesapeake Bay with Corinne. She feels fortunate to wake up and watch the sun rise as eagles and osprey soar overhead. The views of the water are a favorite when family and friends visit from North Carolina, New Jersey, Wisconsin, Canada, South Africa, and Washington, D.C. Summers are spent on the deck overlooking the Bay, enjoying cool summer breezes. Of course, no one can visit Maryland and not eat crabs or oysters. Preparing them fresh from the Bay takes time; it's well worth the effort.

When she isn't enjoying life on the Bay, Kate can be found jogging along the steep surrounding hills or tending to her garden. Weather permitting, she also enjoys kayaking.

Not to be forgotten, Kate gets satisfaction from volunteering at food banks, women's shelters, and for Meals on Wheels.

Contact her at katewinnauthor@gmail.com

www.ingramcontent.com/pod-product-compliance
Lightning Source LLC
Chambersburg PA
CBHW040722100426
42735CB00044B/3451